The Philippines

The Philippines

BY WALTER OLEKSY

Enchantment of the World™
Second Series

CHILDREN'S PRESS®

An Imprint of Scholastic Inc.

New York   Toronto   London   Auckland   Sydney
Mexico City   New Delhi   Hong Kong
Danbury, Connecticut

Frontispiece: **Farmer and mountains on Luzon**

Acknowledgments: I am grateful for the assistance of the following while researching this book: Consul General Leo Herrera-Lim and his staff at the Embassy of the Philippines in Chicago, Illinois; Consul General Jose L. Cuisia Jr. and his staff at the Embassy of the Philippines in Washington, D.C.; and Maria Gonzales-Angelo of Chicago, Illinois, who helped me set up interviews with people in the Philippines.

Consultant: Federico Magdalena, PhD, Associate Director & Faculty Affiliate, Center for Philippine Studies & Asian Studies Program, University of Hawaii at Manoa
Please note: All statistics are as up-to-date as possible at the time of publication.

Book production by The Design Lab

Library of Congress Cataloging-in-Publication Data
Oleksy, Walter G., 1930–
 The Philippines / by Walter Oleksy.
   pages cm. — (Enchantment of the world. Second series)
 Includes bibliographical references and index.
 ISBN 978-0-531-20790-1 (lib. bdg.)
 1. Philippines—Juvenile literature. I. Title.
 DS655.O433 2015
 959.9—dc23   2014001864

1 2 3 4 5 6 7 8 9 10 R 24 23 22 21 20 19 18 17 16 15

Dinagyang festival

Contents

CHAPTER 1   Beautiful Islands **8**

CHAPTER 2   Green Necklace **14**

CHAPTER 3   The Wild World **32**

CHAPTER 4   Island History **42**

CHAPTER 5   Governing the Republic **66**

CHAPTER 6   Making a Living **78**

CHAPTER 7   Living and Learning **86**

CHAPTER 8   Spiritual Life **94**

CHAPTER 9   Culture, Arts, and Sports **102**

CHAPTER 10   Philippine Ways **116**

Timeline **128**

Fast Facts **130**

To Find Out More **134**

Index **136**

Left to right:
Palawan, family on motorbike, lighting candles, rainy day, Mayon Volcano

CHAPTER 1

Beautiful Islands

THE PHILIPPINES IS A TROPICAL LAND IN THE southwestern Pacific Ocean. It has been called the Pearl of the Orient Sea because of the natural beauty of its string of 7,107 islands that looks like a necklace of gems set in the vast blue sea. The islands are a combination of rugged mountains, lush farmland, and white sandy beaches.

The nation of the Philippines is slightly larger than the U.S. state of Arizona. Arizona has a population of only about 6.5 million. The Philippines, on the other hand, was home to 98,734,798 people in 2013, making it the twelfth most-populated country in the world. It has many large, bustling cities, including Manila, the nation's capital, which are crowded with cars, buses, and people.

Opposite: **Boats sit on a beautiful beach on Palawan Island.**

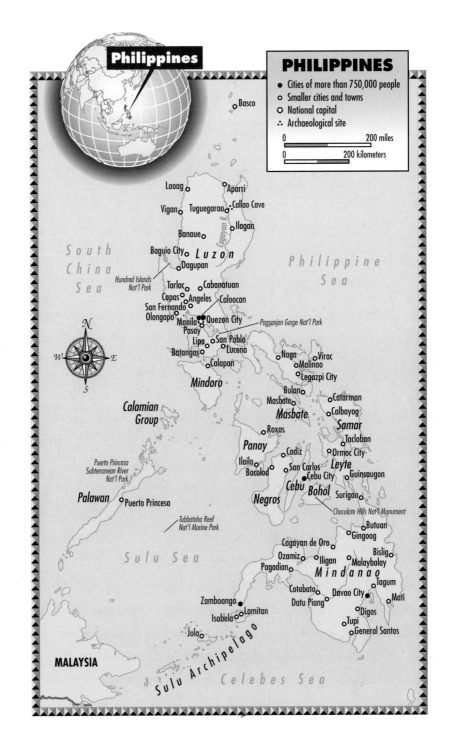

Philippines

PHILIPPINES

- Cities of more than 750,000 people
- Smaller cities and towns
- National capital
- Archaeological site

0   200 miles

0   200 kilometers

Basco

Laoag

Aparri

Vigan

Tuguegarao

Callao Cave

Ilagan

Banaue

Cagayan R.

South China Sea

Baguio City

Luzon

Dagupan

Philippine Sea

Hundred Islands Nat'l Park

Tarlac

Cabanatuan

Capas

Angeles

Caloocan

San Fernando

Olongapo

Manila

Quezon City

Pasay

Pagsanjan Gorge Nat'l Park

Lipa

San Pablo

Batangas

Lucena

Calapan

Naga

Virac

Malinao

Legazpi City

Mindoro

Bulan

Masbate

Catarman

Calamian Group

Masbate

Calbayog

Samar

Roxas

Tacloban

Panay

Cadiz

Ormoc City

Puerto Princesa Subterranean River Nat'l Park

Iloilo

Bacolod

San Carlos

Leyte

Cebu City

Guinsaugon

Palawan

Puerto Princesa

Negros

Cebu

Bohol

Surigao

Chocolate Hills Nat'l Monument

Tubbataha Reef Nat'l Marine Park

Butuan

Gingoog

Sulu Sea

Cagayan de Oro

Ozamiz

Bislig

Pagadian

Iligan

Malaybalay

Mindanao

Tagum

Cotabato

Davao City

Mati

Datu Piang

Zamboanga

Digos

Isabela

Lamitan

Tupi

General Santos

Jolo

Sulu Archipelago

MALAYSIA

Celebes Sea

N / *S* / *E* / *W*

The people of the Philippines come from about a hundred different ethnic groups, and they speak an equal number of different languages. Many are descended from Malay people who migrated to the Philippine islands thousands of years ago. Europeans first arrived in the Philippines in the 1500s. Spain claimed the Philippines as its own and ruled it for more than three hundred years. The United States took over in 1898, and in 1946, the Philippines became a completely independent nation.

A T'boli woman in traditional dress. The T'boli people live in the central part of the island of Mindanao.

In the years since, the country has confronted natural disasters, corruption, and dictators. Yet it has also moved boldly into the modern world, with a growing economy, a strong education system, and one of the most computer-literate populations in the world.

Some things have not changed, however. Filipinos today maintain their long-standing reputation for being among the world's friendliest people.

High-rise office buildings line the streets in Makati, the financial center of the Philippines. Makati is one of sixteen cities that make up the metropolitan region of Manila.

Saving the Flag

Filipinos are called some of the most patriotic people on the planet. One Filipino girl demonstrated this when Typhoon Juaning slammed into the Philippines in 2011.

Janela Arcos Lelis, a small twelve-year-old, waded through floodwaters up to her chest in the town of Malinao on the island of Luzon, risking her life to save the Philippine flag. Her country's national symbol was in danger of being swept away. Nine people, including three children, died in floodwaters that day.

Janela's house had been submerged in the flood, so Janela had taken shelter in a neighbor's house. Janela's brother was on his way to try to evacuate relatives from houses nearby, when he stopped by to tell Janela to save the flag, which his school had entrusted to him. It was on a pole, leaning against a wall in the corner of the living room.

Though she could have drowned, Janela immediately went into the house to retrieve the flag. Wading through the chest-high waters, she picked up the flag and brought it out of the house. "When I reached the flooded street," Janela said later, "I held the flag above the water. I also held on tightly to a rope that our village captain had set up for evacuating the town, so I wasn't swept away by the floodwaters in the streets that were like fast-moving rivers."

Albay resident Frank Lurzano took a picture of Janela carrying the flag in the flooded streets of Malinao. The dramatic photo ran on front pages of local newspapers after the flood, and her heroic act became worldwide news. She was called a national hero for doing what soldiers on a battlefield will do—risk their lives to save their country's flag.

CHAPTER 2

Green Necklace

THE PHILIPPINES IS AN ARCHIPELAGO, OR A CHAIN of islands. Sometimes called the Green Necklace of the Pacific, it consists of 7,107 lush green islands stretching across the blue of the western Pacific Ocean.

The Philippines is a rich land. Its islands are crowded with towering mountains, clear lakes, secluded beaches and dramatic cliffs. It boasts explosive volcanoes, charming villages, and exciting and very modern cities.

Opposite: **Palawan includes a sparsely settled string of islands that stretches westward across the blue sea toward Malaysia.**

In the Sea

Several different sections of the Pacific Ocean surround the Philippine archipelago. The South China Sea lies to the west, the Sulu Sea to the southwest, the Celebes Sea lies to the south, and the Philippine Sea to the east. The 200-mile-wide (320 kilometer) Luzon Strait lies directly north of the Philippines, and north of the strait lies Taiwan. Other nearby nations include Malaysia, Indonesia, and Vietnam.

The Philippine islands run about 1,150 miles (1,850 km) from north to south. Combined, the islands cover about 120,000 square miles (310,000 sq km) of land. This makes the Philippines the sixty-fourth largest country in the world. But because it is made up of islands, it has one of the world's longest coastlines, measuring about 22,000 miles (35,000 km).

Sandy beaches line much of the coastline in the Philippines.

Geographic Features of the Philippines

Area: About 120,000 square miles (310,000 sq km)

Number of Islands: 7,107

Largest Island: Luzon, 40,420 square miles (104,687 sq km)

Highest Elevation: Mount Apo, 9,692 feet (2,954 m)

Lowest Elevation: Sea level along the coasts

Longest River: Cagayan River, Luzon, 220 miles (354 km)

Largest Lake: Laguna de Bay, Luzon, 356 square miles (922 sq km)

Average High Temperature: In Manila, 86°F (30°C) in January, 94°F (34°C) in May

Average Low Temperature: In Manila, 70°F (21°C) in January, 76°F (24°C) in June

Average Annual Rainfall: 35 to 216 inches (89 to 549 cm) per year

Although the Philippines is made up of thousands of islands, 95 percent of the country's total land area lies in just eleven of them. These major islands can be divided into three groups. The Luzon group lies at the northern end of the archipelago. This group includes the island of Luzon, the largest island in the Philippines, along with Mindoro and Palawan. In the center of the archipelago is the Visayas group. Bohol, Cebu, Leyte, Masbate, Negros, Panay, and Samar are the major islands in this group. The third group is Mindanao, the second-largest island in the Philippines. Many of the small Philippine islands are remote and uninhabited. Some of the small islands don't have names.

Houses perch atop a mountain ridge in the central part of Luzon Island.

A Mountainous Land

Mountains tower atop the islands that make up the Philippines. The Cordillera Central is the main mountain chain on Luzon. This range includes Mount Pulag, the nation's third-highest mountain, which reaches an elevation of 9,587 feet (2,922 meters). Other ranges on Luzon include the Caraballo Mountains and the Zambales Mountains.

The island of Mindanao also features several mountain ranges, including the Diwata on the east coast and the Butig in the west. It also boasts the two highest mountains in the nation. Rugged Mount Dulang-dulang in the north-central part of the island reaches 9,649 feet (2,941 m), while Mount Apo in the south towers at 9,692 feet (2,954 m).

Mount Apo towers over the coastline in southeastern Mindanao.

Chocolate Hills

The island of Bohol in the Visayas group is home to one of the most spectacular sites in the Philippines. The Chocolate Hills consist of 1,268 perfectly cone-shaped hills rising about 100 to 160 feet (30 to 50 m) high. Their name comes from the fact that they look like chocolate candies when the grass that covers them turns brown in the dry season. These unusual hills, made of eroded limestone, have become one of the nation's top tourist attractions.

On all the islands, the land slopes down from the mountains to farming terraces, where people have cut into the mountainsides to make level land that can be farmed. From

Farming terraces in central Luzon

there, the land continues to drop to plains. Along the coast are narrow lowlands, which end in some of the most beautiful beaches in the world. Some of these beaches are pristine paradises in remote locations. Others have been developed with large resorts and many fine hotels and restaurants.

Some Philippine resorts include thatched-roof cottages where visitors sleep above the gentle waves.

Rivers and Lakes

Water is abundant in the Philippines. Rivers rush down the mountains to the sea. The nation's longest rivers are the Cagayan River in northern Luzon and the Agusan River in eastern Mindanao. The 120-mile (190 km) Pampanga River, which flows across Luzon into Manila Bay, is another vital waterway.

The largest lake in the Philippines is Laguna de Bay, which spreads out across 356 square miles (922 sq km) in central Luzon near Manila. Other major lakes include Lake Lanao, on Mindanao, and Taal Lake, which sits in an old volcanic crater on the island of Luzon.

Taal Volcano is located on a large island in Taal Lake. Inside the volcano's crater is a smaller lake called Main Crater Lake, which contains a small island called Vulcan Point. Vulcan Point is the world's largest island in a lake (Main Crater Lake) on an island (Taal Island) in a lake (Taal Lake) on an island (Luzon).

Climate

There are two distinct seasons in the Philippines, the wet season and the dry season. These seasons are largely the result of the monsoons, or the prevailing winds. During the wet season, which runs from June to October, the monsoon winds carry in wet air from the southwest. During the dry season, from November to May, the winds shift and come from the northeast.

In Manila, January is the coolest month, with daytime temperatures reaching a high of around 86 degrees Fahrenheit (30 degrees Celsius), while April and May are the hottest, with the average daily temperature peaking at 94°F (34°C). The eastern part of the island chain receives the most rain, with more than 160 inches (400 centimeters) falling in many places. Manila, on the other hand, receives only 87 inches (221 cm) per year.

Typhoons

Typhoons are a threat during the wet season, causing canceled flights, flooded roads, and, sometimes, devastated towns. These fierce storms, also called tropical cyclones, have sustained winds of at least 73 miles per hour (118 kph) and carry lashing rain. An average of nineteen typhoons approach the Philippine archipelago each year, but usually only eight or nine make landfall.

In the Philippines, typhoons are called *bagyo*. They are named after Baguio City, the site of the wettest typhoon in Philippine history. This storm poured 87 inches (221 cm) of rain on the city over the course of four days in 1911.

Super Typhoon Haiyan struck the country's eastern seaboard in November 2013. Haiyan was one of the strongest typhoons in world history. More than 6,100 people were killed in the storm, most of them in and around the city of Tacloban, the capital of the province of Leyte, about 360 miles (580 km) southeast of Manila, the country's capital. Another 23,500 or more Filipinos were injured, and about 1,700 others were missing. The typhoon left behind a catastrophic scene after it made landfall on six Philippine islands, flattening some communities and displacing more than four million people.

Tropical cyclones do not have to reach typhoon strength to cause significant damage. One of the deadliest storms in Philippine history was Tropical Storm Thelma, which had sustained winds of only about 45 miles per hour (72 kph). It blew into the Philippines on November 5, 1991, and pummeled the islands for about twenty-four hours. Thelma killed more than five

Typhoon Haiyan damaged or destroyed more than a million houses in the Philippines.

thousand people, most of them in Ormoc City on Leyte Island. The city was flooded with little warning. More than three thousand other people were missing and presumed dead. About 4,500 homes were destroyed and another 22,000 were badly damaged.

Tsunamis

Another type of natural disaster that sometimes strikes the Philippines is a tsunami. A tsunami occurs when a large volume of water is displaced in the ocean, often because of an earthquake. This causes a series of waves that can grow to towering heights when they reach land.

Residents inspect their destroyed neighborhood after flooding in Ormoc City in 1991.

The worst tsunami in Philippine history struck a wide area of Mindanao on August 17, 1976, following a powerful earthquake. Thousands of people who were asleep when the tsunami hit were swept away by waves 15 feet (4.5 m) high and died without knowing what hit them. Together, the earthquake and tsunami killed about eight thousand people and injured thousands of others. They also destroyed hundreds of homes and other buildings. It was the deadliest disaster the Philippines has experienced to date.

To help save lives in the event of these natural disasters, tsunami detectors and better, faster alert sirens have been installed throughout the Philippines. The nation is always working to improve its methods for preparing for natural disasters. "Our goal is to develop more ways to protect the Filipino people from natural calamities," proclaimed President Benigno S. Aquino III in 2013.

Scientists at the Philippine Institute of Volcanology and Seismology carefully monitor earthquake activity so they can warn Filipinos of potentially dangerous tsunamis.

Deadly Nature

Here are the ten deadliest natural disasters in Philippine history:

1. A magnitude 7.9 earthquake set off a tsunami that struck the island of Mindanao on August 17, 1976. The combined events killed about 8,000 people.

2. Super Typhoon Haiyan made landfall in the Philippines on November 8, 2013. It killed more than 6,100 people, mostly on Leyte Island. Another 1,700 went missing.

3. Tropical Storm Thelma caused flash floods in Ormoc City on Leyte Island on November 5, 1991. More than 5,100 people died.

4. Typhoon Bopha smashed into the island of Mindanao on December 3, 2012. More than 1,900 people died, and another 800 went missing.

5. A magnitude 7.8 earthquake shook Baguio City and other parts of the northern Philippines on July 16, 1990, killing 1,621 people (left).

6. Typhoon Ike blew across the central islands on August 31, 1984, killing 1,363 people.

7. Taal Volcano on the island of Luzon erupted on January 30, 1911, killing about 1,300 people.

8. Tropical Storm Washi slammed into Mindanao island on December 16, 2011, killing more than 1,200 people.

9. Mayon Volcano in the eastern part of Luzon erupted on February 1, 1814. About 1,200 people died.

10. A massive landslide buried the village of Guinsaugon on the island of Leyte on February 17, 2006, killing 1,126 people (above).

Volcanoes and Earthquakes

The Philippines is located along the Ring of Fire, an area around the edge of the Pacific Ocean where the vast majority of Earth's strong earthquakes and volcanic eruptions occur. The worst eruption in the Philippines in recorded history occurred in 1991. Mount Pinatubo, on the island of Luzon, had not erupted since long before the arrival of the Spaniards. At that time, it was covered with dense forest and farmland. The long-sleeping mountain came violently awake on June 15, 1991. It blew its top, throwing massive amounts of ash

The eruption of Mount Pinatubo in 1991 was Earth's largest volcanic eruption in the twentieth century. It sent so much ash and other material into the atmosphere that it cooled the globe about 0.9°F (0.5°C).

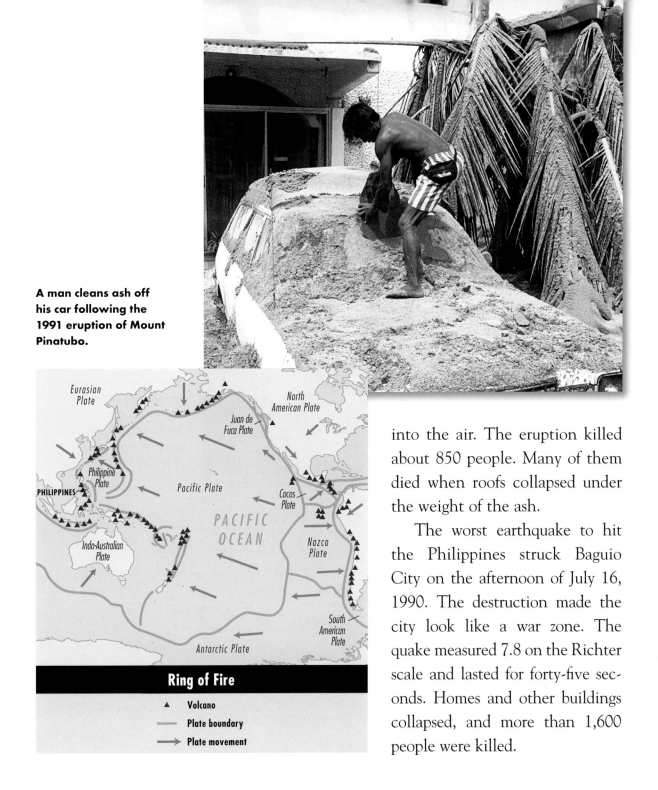

A man cleans ash off his car following the 1991 eruption of Mount Pinatubo.

Ring of Fire

▲ Volcano

— Plate boundary

→ Plate movement

Eurasian Plate

North American Plate

Juan de Fuca Plate

Philippine Plate

PHILIPPINES

Pacific Plate

Cocos Plate

PACIFIC OCEAN

Nazca Plate

Indo-Australian Plate

South American Plate

Antarctic Plate

into the air. The eruption killed about 850 people. Many of them died when roofs collapsed under the weight of the ash.

The worst earthquake to hit the Philippines struck Baguio City on the afternoon of July 16, 1990. The destruction made the city look like a war zone. The quake measured 7.8 on the Richter scale and lasted for forty-five seconds. Homes and other buildings collapsed, and more than 1,600 people were killed.

Looking at Philippine Cities

The largest and richest city in the Philippines is Quezon City, which has a population of about 2.7 million. It is located in Metropolitan Manila, or Metro Manila, the national capital region on the island of Luzon. Quezon City was named after Manuel L. Quezon, who served as president of the Philippines from 1935 to 1944. In 1938, Quezon began pushing for a city to replace Manila as the nation's capital, arguing that Manila was too crowded and vulnerable to attack from the sea. Quezon City was founded in 1939 and served as the national capital from 1948 until 1976. The House of Representatives, one of the houses in the Philippine Congress, is still located in Quezon City. The Senate is in Manila. Today, many of the nation's TV stations are based in Quezon City. The main campuses of two of the nation's largest universities, the Ateneo de Manila University and the University of the Philippines Diliman, are also located in the city.

The capital city of Manila is the nation's second-largest city, with a population of more than 1.6 million. The third-largest city, Caloocan, is also part of the Metro Manila area and has a population of about 1.5 million. The city was a center of the Philippine revolution against the Spanish in the 1890s. Its best-known monument is on the site of the first battle of the revolution and honors the revolutionary leader Andres Bonifacio.

Davao City, the Philippines' fourth-largest city, is home to nearly 1.5 million people. Located on the island of Mindanao, it is the island's center of business and industry. It was founded as a Christian settlement by Spanish conqueror José Cruz de Uyanguren in 1848 and as a city in 1936. Davao City is an ethnic melting pot, attracting migrants from around the country. Its inhabitants speak Tagalog, English, Cebuano, Chinese, and, to a lesser extent, Japanese. The highest mountain

in the country, Mount Apo, is located in Davao.

Cebu City, the nation's fifth-largest city, was home to nearly 900,000 people in 2010. Located on the eastern shore of Cebu Island, in the Visayas, Cebu City was founded as the first Spanish settlement in 1575. Today, Cebu City is one of the country's main ports and an important center of industry. It is also a popular tourist destination. One of its best-known sites is Magellan's Cross (above), which Ferdinand Magellan's crew planted in the ground when they arrived in the Philippines in 1521. The cross now standing is likely a replica erected after the original disintegrated. Not far from the cross is the Church of the Holy Child, a massive stone church that dates to the 1700s.

CHAPTER 3

The Wild World

T HE PHILIPPINE ISLANDS HAVE RICH VOLCANIC mineral soil and abundant sunshine and rainfall, making them ideal for plant life. The islands' forests and lowlands and lakes and rivers also serve as habitat for a wide array of creatures.

Plant Life

A hundred years ago, the vast majority of the land in the Philippines was covered in forest. Today, after years of logging, mining, and clearing the land for farms and cities, less than 25 percent of the land is covered in forest.

Pine trees are common in the mountains, while giant fig trees and lauan trees grow in the rain forest. Also common in the rain forest are the narra tree, a flowering hardwood, and palm trees. Rattan, a thin, vine-like stem related to the palm, is used to make mats, bags, and hats.

National Flower

The sampaguita, a species of jasmine, is the national flower. Its white flowers are small and star-shaped, and they remain in bloom throughout the year. They open at night and last for about a day. The flowers grow in bunches on the plant, a woody shrub that can grow 5 feet (1.5 m) tall. To Filipinos, the white, sweet-smelling flower represents humility, purity, simplicity, and strength.

Sampaguitas have many uses. The flowers are used to make perfumes as well as teas. They are also strung into garlands that people wear around their necks at festivals or celebrations. Sometimes sampaguitas are used at religious ceremonies as offerings to the gods. Some people hang sampaguita flowers from the mirrors of their cars.

The forests are also filled with thousands of species of smaller plants. Delicate ferns thrive in the wet environment, and flowering plants also abound. More than a thousand different kinds of orchids grow in the Philippines. Many are named after insects and animals, such as the butterfly spider and lizard orchids. The rare waling-waling orchid grows only on the island of Mindanao and is called the queen of the Philippine flowers. Filipinos sometimes welcome visitors with orchid garlands to wear around the neck, much like Hawaiians greet visitors with leis of their native flowers.

Some coastal areas of the Philippines are home to useful trees called mangroves. Unlike most trees, mangroves can grow in saltwater. Mangroves have long, thin roots that rise above the water. The tangle of roots in a mangrove forest

Coconut Palm Trees

One of the most important plants in the Philippines is the coconut palm tree. The islands are the world's largest producer of coconuts, which are both exported and eaten at home. In the Philippines, coconut trees are sometimes called the tree of life because coconuts have so many uses. Coconuts are used to make main dishes, drinks, and desserts. Coconut juice is a popular drink, and coconut milk and grated coconut flakes are used in many recipes. Coconut leaves are sometimes wrapped around rice when it is cooked or stored.

serves as a nursery for young fish and other sea creatures. The mangroves also protect the land from strong waves during storms. When mangroves are cut, the waves easily erode the coastline, and flooding is more common because there are no trees to block the powerful seas. After Super Typhoon Haiyan killed thousands of people in 2013, the Philippine government announced that it would plant mangrove forests to help limit such disasters in the future.

Mammals

More than two hundred species of mammals live in the Philippines. These range from lumbering water buffalo to spry mice. In addition, there are many species of monkeys, lemurs, squirrels, and deer. Other creatures found in the Philippines include wild pigs, civets, leopard cats (small cats named for their leopard-like spots), and bear cats. Less well-known creatures include scaly anteaters called pangolins and tiny deerlike creatures called chevrotains. Also known as mouse deer, chevrotains are often only about 1 foot (30 cm) tall.

About a hundred mammal species are endemic to the Philippines, meaning they are found nowhere else. These include the Philippine tarsier, one of the world's smallest primates. Even as an adult, this tiny tree-dwelling monkey relative is only about the size of a human fist. Another endemic mammal is the tamaraw, a species of small water buffalo that lives only on Mindoro and is famed for its fierceness.

Tarsiers are nocturnal, meaning they are active at night. Their huge eyes help them hunt at night for the insects that make up most of their diet.

Carabao

Huge, hardworking water buffalo called carabao were introduced into the swamps of the Philippines by Malay immigrants more than two thousand years ago. These large ox-like creatures can handle the heat of the Philippines because the islands have abundant water. The animals cool themselves by splashing and rolling around in swamps. They also roll in the mud, coating themselves with the gray muck. This helps keep them cool and fends off insects.

Carabao are the most important domestic animals in the Philippines today. On the islands' farms, they pull ploughs through fields of rice. They also are used like trucks, pulling carts with heavy loads that need to be moved from one place to another. Carabao are also a source of meat, milk, and hide for Filipino farmers. Centuries ago their thick skin was used to make armor for Filipino warriors. In 2013, there were nearly three million carabao in the Philippines, most of them on small farms.

More than fifty different types of bats live in the Philippines, and many live nowhere else. Bats unique to the Philippines include the giant golden-crowned flying fox, one of the world's largest bats. These creatures, which have a wingspan of more than 5 feet (1.5 m), live only in the forest, away from people. They live on wild fruit, especially figs.

Reptiles and Birds

About 270 species of reptiles are found in the Philippines. Among them are more than a hundred kinds of snakes, including some of the most fearsome snakes in world. The

Philippine crocodiles have sixty-six to sixty-eight teeth. Their teeth are constantly growing, and if they fall out new ones will grow in.

king cobra, the longest venomous snake in the world, is found on Palawan. It can reach 18 feet (5.5 m) in length. Pythons are even larger, sometimes reaching 30 feet (9 m). They are not venomous. They kill prey by biting it and then winding themselves around the creature and squeezing. Brightly colored venomous pit vipers live in trees, while kraits patrol the waters. These venomous water snakes can be found in rivers and lakes. Some species even live in the ocean.

Another fearsome Philippine reptile is the Philippine crocodile. This freshwater crocodile grows about 10 feet (3 m) long and eats fish, shrimp, snakes, birds, and small mammals. These crocodiles are severely endangered. Only about 250 of them still exist in the wild, mainly on Luzon and other northern Philippine islands.

Small lizards called geckos are much less threatening. They are welcome in many Filipino homes because they keep the house free of insects. Children often keep geckos as pets.

Common birds in the Philippines include cockatoos, hawks, mallards, whistling ducks, owls, and pigeons. The largest bird in the islands is the sarus crane, which stands up to 6 feet (1.8 m) tall. That's about as tall as an adult man. The world's smallest falcon, the Philippine falconet, or pygmy falcon, is also found in the islands. It is only about 6 inches (15 cm) tall.

The sarus crane is the world's tallest flying bird.

National Bird

The Philippine eagle is the national bird of the Philippines. This shaggy-headed creature is one of the most powerful birds in the world. It is a major predator in the Philippine forest. It hunts whatever is available, including lemurs, monkeys, civets, bats, rats, reptiles, and other birds.

Philippine eagles are critically endangered now, mainly because cutting down forests has destroyed their habitat. Today, only a few hundred remain. Because of this, they are protected in the Philippines. A person who kills one of these birds can be sent to jail for twelve years.

Green sea turtles are one of the many species that live in Philippine waters.

Life in Water

Fish is a main source of protein for the people of the Philippines. Hundreds of species of fish that swim in the seas around the island are suitable for eating. These include tuna, herring, mackerel, grouper, swordfish, sea bass, anchovies, and sardines.

Many visitors to the Philippines go snorkeling or diving to get a good look at the amazing sea life. They might see rays, eels, sharks, lionfish, and much more. The seas also hold dolphins, whales, jellyfish, sea anemones, sponges, and starfish.

The Philippines is a paradise for shell collectors, with more than twenty-one thousand of the world's one hundred thousand shellfish species found in the archipelago. Filipinos dive for them in the seas or find them on the beaches.

Filipinos sell seashells and starfish at a beach on Cebu Island.

Sometimes they turn the shells into jewelry. The shells also are sold to visitors or for export. The rarest of them may be worth thousands of dollars.

Tubbataha Reef

One of the most magnificent coral reefs in the world lies in the Sulu Sea, about 100 miles (160 km) south of Palawan Island. Tubbataha Reef National Marine Park includes two small islands and some spectacular underwater reefs. More than six hundred fish species live around the reef. That's 40 percent of all the species of reef fish in the world! In addition, the reef provides habitat for dolphins, whales, birds, and nesting hawksbill and green sea turtles.

Tubbataha is considered one of the best scuba diving spots in the world. There are no tourist facilities at the reef, so visitors have to sleep on boats. But Tubbataha is so beautiful that many of the boats are booked years in advance. The reef is a Philippine national treasure and appears on the 1,000 peso bill.

CHAPTER 4

Island History

N 2007, ARCHAEOLOGISTS, PEOPLE WHO STUDY THE remains of past human life, discovered a small bone from a human toe in Callao Cave in northern Luzon. When scientists dated the bone, they found that it was from a man who had died about sixty-seven thousand years earlier. This man, now known as Callao Man, is the earliest-known human to live in the Philippines archipelago. Callao Man was short, probably less than 4 feet (1.2 m) tall. His descendants are believed to be living today among the Aetas, people who live in the mountains of the island of Luzon.

Opposite: **Aeta hunters aim arrows in a photograph from 1953. The Aetas are thought to be the descendants of Callao Man.**

Life on the Islands

Experts are not certain where the earliest people to settle in the Philippines came from. They likely arrived in waves from various parts of Southeast Asia over the centuries.

Banaue Rice Terraces

Two thousand years ago, farmers in a region called Ifugao in the central part of the island of Luzon carved massive rice terraces into the mountainsides. There are several clusters of these terraces in Ifugao, but the most famous is in Banaue.

Using few tools other than their hands, the ancient people of this region moved mountains to create the terraces, which step thousands of feet up the hillsides. They built walls to capture the water and create the ponds in which the rice grows. These fields have been passed down through families for generations, and many are still in use.

The people of the Philippines hunted, fished, and farmed. By two thousand years ago, people were cutting terraces into the mountains of Luzon to grow rice. In the coastal areas, people lived in groups called *barangays*, which were ruled by *datus*, or chieftains. Each barangay probably had only a few hundred people in it. The early people of the Philippines followed many different religions. Some worshipped one god, and some worshipped many gods.

By the 900s CE, people in the Philippines were in contact with Chinese traders. Trade with other Asian people soon followed. In the 1400s, Muslims, followers of the religion Islam, arrived in the Philippines from the south. The religion was spreading throughout the Philippines when Europeans first came to the islands.

Europeans Arrive

A Spanish expedition anchored at Cebu Island in 1521. The five ships were under the command of a Portuguese explorer named Ferdinand Magellan. A few weeks after arriving in the Philippines, Magellan was trying to convert a chieftain on the island of Mactan to Christianity. After the chief refused, a battle broke out between the Spaniards and the locals. Magellan died in the fight, and his crew left the Philippines without establishing a settlement.

Ferdinand Magellan died on April 27, 1521, in a battle with Filipinos.

The Spanish conquest of the Philippines began in earnest in 1565 during an expedition by Spanish conquistador Miguel López de Legazpi, who established a fort and a Catholic church on the island of Cebu. This was the first Spanish settlement in the Philippines. By 1569, the Spanish settlement in Cebu had become an important port for ships and a starting point for further exploration of the archipelago.

Three years after de Legazpi's arrival, a Portuguese fleet arrived to challenge his rule but was unsuccessful. Legazpi then moved northward and established the city of Manila in 1571.

Around the World

On September 20, 1519, Ferdinand Magellan set sail from Spain, with five ships carrying about 270 men. The expedition, which was funded by the Spanish Crown, was searching for a westward route to Asia. The ships sailed across the Atlantic Ocean and around the southern tip of South America. From there, they set out across the Pacific, arriving in the Philippine archipelago in March 1521. Magellan died in the Philippines, but the expedition continued on without him under the leadership of Juan Sebastián del Cano (right).

On September 9, 1522, del Cano arrived back in Spain with just one ship and eighteen men. All the other men had died on the journey. It had taken three years and many lives, but these explorers were the first people to circumnavigate—go completely around—the globe.

Spanish Rule

Legazpi's efforts began an era of Spanish colonization that lasted for more than three centuries. He became the first Spanish governor-general of the Philippines, the person in charge of the islands. Legazpi City, the capital of the province of Albay, was named in his honor.

Spanish rule introduced Christianity to the Philippines. People across the islands were converted, at least in name, to the Roman Catholic religion. Many people who lived on the southern islands of Mindanao and Sulu, however, remained Muslim.

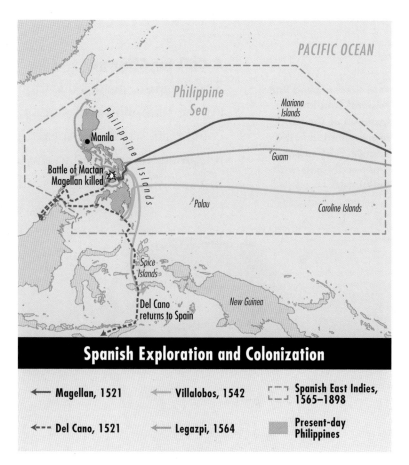

Spanish Exploration and Colonization

← Magellan, 1521   ← Villalobos, 1542   Spanish East Indies, 1565–1898

←-- Del Cano, 1521   ← Legazpi, 1564   Present-day Philippines

The church had tremendous power during the colonial period. The archbishop, the leading religious figure in the islands, was the second most-powerful person there after the governor-general. The church built hospitals and schools. Priests all over the islands worked to make the people actively Catholic and prevent them from taking part in their old religions. The old ways died hard, however, and many people mixed Catholic traditions with their older religious traditions.

A Call for Change

José Rizal argued that Filipinos should have freedom of speech, representation in the Spanish parliament, and equal rights with Spaniards.

The Spanish made education free for all Filipinos in 1863. At the time, however, only a small portion of the population could read, write, and speak Spanish. Education in the islands remained limited, and in the late 1800s, many wealthy people in the Philippines began sending their children to Europe to be educated. Many of these young people became more nationalistic and wanted to change Philippine society. The most prominent of these people was José Rizal.

Rizal is considered one of the Philippines' greatest national heroes. He was a physician, scientist, poet, and novelist. His novels were very influential in the Philippines and encouraged nationalism. In 1892, Rizal returned to the Philippines, where he argued for moderate reforms. Although he did not recommend becoming independent from Spain, the Spanish arrested him anyway. He was executed by firing squad in 1896.

Fort Santiago

Built in 1571, Fort Santiago is the oldest Spanish fortress in the Philippines. Spanish conqueror Miguel López de Legazpi had the fort built to defend the newly established city of Manila. The massive stone structure has walls that are 8 feet (2.4 m) thick and 22 feet (6.7 m) high. The fort suffered heavy damage during World War II, but remains a popular attraction. One of the most popular attractions at the fort is the Rizal Shrine, the prison cell that held the national hero José Rizal. The last footsteps Rizal took on the way to his execution are indicated on the fort's floor. There is also a museum about Rizal's life.

Revolt

A secret independence movement group called the Katipunan was formed in 1892. Its members were dedicated to ending Spanish rule in the islands. In August 1896, the Philippine Revolution began. Rebels and Spanish forces clashed near Manila.

Two years later, war broke out between Spain and the United States. The Spanish-American War was centered in Cuba, an island in the Caribbean Sea only about 90 miles (145 km) from Florida, but the Americans also sent warships to the Philippines.

In the Philippines, rebel leader Emilio Aguinaldo declared independence from Spain on June 12, 1898. The following year, he was named president of the First Philippine Republic.

Meanwhile, the Spanish-American War had ended. In December 1898, Spain and the United States signed the

Treaty of Paris. Under this treaty, Spain ceded the Philippines to the United States in exchange for $20 million.

But the Filipinos wanted independence. They didn't want to replace one colonial ruler with another. The Americans, however, did not accept Philippine independence, and fighting broke out between U.S. and Philippine forces. The Americans defeated the rebels.

Emilio Aguinaldo was a leader in the Philippine fight for independence against both Spain and the United States.

The American Years

The United States set up a colonial government in 1900. But many Americans were opposed to the United States being an imperial power. So instead, U.S. officials began saying that they were training the Filipinos with the goal that the Philippines would eventually become independent. In the following years, the American role in the Philippine government declined. Although the governor-general, the leading official in the islands, was American, gradually more and more of the other government officials were Filipino.

During the 1920s and 1930s, Americans and Filipinos alike put tremendous energy into improving education in the Philippines. Thousands of Filipino teachers were trained, and half of the government budget went to education. By the 1930s, about half the Philippine population could read and write.

American forces advance across a field during the Philippine-American War in 1899.

Manuel Quezon served as president from 1935 to 1944. Following the Japanese invasion in 1941, however, he led the government while in exile in the United States.

In 1935, the Philippines became an autonomous commonwealth of the United States, meaning it was a self-governing region that was still under U.S. power. The United States remained in charge of the Philippines' defense and foreign affairs. Manuel Quezon was elected the new republic's first president. Under his leadership, Philippine women gained the right to vote, and he began making economic reforms. The United States had agreed that the Philippines would

achieve complete independence in ten years. Philippine independence soon took a backseat to greater concerns, however, as rumblings of war were heard throughout the region and around the world.

Japanese prime minister Hideki Tojo salutes Japanese troops on a visit to the Philippines in 1943. Japan occupied the Philippines for three years during World War II.

World War II

Japan invaded China in 1937 and in the following years became increasingly threatening toward its neighbors in East Asia. By 1939, war had also started in Europe, with the United Kingdom, France, and other countries battling Germany and its allies, but the United States was not yet involved. Then, on December 7, 1941, Japan bombed the U.S. naval base at Pearl Harbor, Hawaii. Just a few hours later, Japanese forces attacked the Philippines. Japanese troops gained control of Manila on January 2, 1942.

Filipinos fought heroically against the Japanese alongside U.S. troops under the command of U.S. general Douglas MacArthur, attempting to defend Bataan Peninsula on Luzon Island and nearby Corregidor Island. However, the Japanese prevented the Philippine and American troops from receiving much needed supplies, forcing them to surrender.

In 1943, the Japanese helped set up the Second Philippine Republic. The president of the republic, José Laurel, was chosen by the Japanese.

The war in the Pacific was not going well for the United States and the other Allies. In March 1942, MacArthur was ordered to Australia, but he promised the Filipinos, "I shall return." He continued efforts to take their islands back from the Japanese and made good on his promise to return by arriving by ship at Leyte, an island in the eastern Visayas, with an invasion force of 174,000 troops in October 1944. Americans and Filipinos were soon back in control of the Philippines.

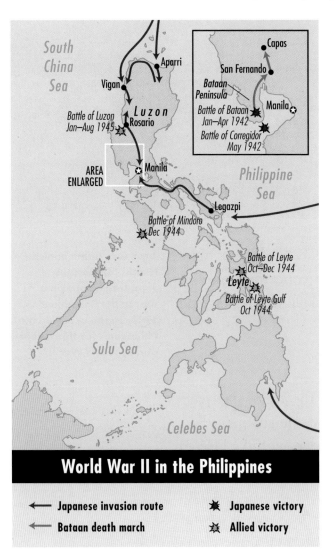

World War II in the Philippines

← Japanese invasion route
← Bataan death march
✳ Japanese victory
✳ Allied victory

Bataan Death March

One of the worst events in the Philippines during World War II was the fall of Bataan to the Japanese in April 1942. Between 350 and 400 Filipino officers and soldiers surrendered, but were executed. Then between 90,000 and 100,000 American and Filipino soldiers were taken prisoner. Starting on the southern end of the Bataan Peninsula on April 9, they were forced to march 55 miles (89 km) over high desert terrain to a city called San Fernando. They were then loaded into boxcars and taken by train to the town of Capas. From there, they walked a final 8 miles (13 km) to a prisoner of war camp called Camp O'Donnell.

Along the way, the prisoners were starved, kicked, and beaten. Some of those who fell, too exhausted to keep walking in the hot sun without water, were stabbed with bayonets. Between 7,000 and 10,000 of the prisoners died along the way.

The Bataan Death March was called a war crime. A court ruled that General Masaharu Homma had permitted his troops in the Philippines to commit "brutal atrocities and other high crimes" and he was executed by firing squad in 1946, outside Manila.

Independence and Rebellion

The United States granted the Philippines complete independence on July 4, 1946. The Third Republic of the Philippines was established with Manila as the capital and Manuel Roxas as its first president. Roxas had been a hero in the war, serving bravely as part of an underground Manila intelligence group.

Huk rebels in a jail in 1951. The Huks began as a resistance movement against the Japanese during World War II, and their name is an abbreviation of words meaning the People's Anti-Japanese Army.

Independence did not, however, bring political or economic stability to the new nation. Political unrest and poverty followed the war. At the time, most Filipinos were poor. Many were tenant farmers who worked other people's land on vast estates. The poor farmers lived in desperate poverty and were growing increasingly angry at the wealthy estate owners.

Some of these peasants banded together in what is known as the Hukbalahap, or Huk, Rebellion. The Huk leaders were communists. Their goal was to take over the estates and divide them into smaller parcels to be given to poor farmers. The Huks operated out of central Luzon, and in the years after independence they became increasingly powerful. When Philippine officials attempted to crush them, they only became more popular. Eventually, however, many of the Huk leaders were arrested. Concerned about the spread of communism, the U.S. government gave more military supplies to Philippine authorities. Philippine forces finally defeated the Huks in 1954.

The Young Nation

In the early years of Philippine independence, the country struggled to establish an honest and effective government. President Roxas had died in 1948 and was succeeded by his vice president, Elpidio Quirino. Corruption was widespread under Quirino's government. During his six years in office, however, the country's economy improved.

In 1953, a Philippine congressman, Ramon Magsaysay, became president. During his years as president, he reduced

Ramon Magsaysay (second from right) campaigns for president in 1953. As secretary of defense in the early 1950s, Magsaysay had been central in defeating the Huk movement.

corruption and supported a labor movement. His death in a plane crash in 1957 was deeply mourned by Filipinos. He was succeeded by Carlos Garcia, whose administration was also perceived as corrupt.

In 1961, Diosdado Macapagal became president. He worked to improve the economy. He also tried to improve the lot of poor farmers and lessen government corruption. He was frequently at odds with the conservative Congress, however, and in 1965, he lost his bid for reelection to the president of the Senate, Ferdinand Marcos.

By 1960, Metropolitan Manila was a thriving region, home to more than two million people.

The Marcos Years

Ferdinand Marcos's time in office was marked by great corruption. It was also a time of great social upheaval. Students took to the streets in massive demonstrations, demanding change. Communism was again on the rise. Meanwhile, Muslim Filipinos, known as Moros, demanded independence for the parts of the islands that had large Muslim populations.

In 1972, as Marcos neared the end of his second term as president, he declared martial law, meaning that the military would maintain order. At the time, the Philippine constitution limited presidents to two terms. Under martial law, Marcos jailed his political opponents. Human rights and freedom suffered. The following year, a new constitution was

Ferdinand Marcos visits U.S. president Richard Nixon in 1969. The United States supported Marcos throughout his career.

About eight hundred pairs of Imelda Marcos's shoes are now part of the Marikina Shoe Museum near Manila.

written. Marcos named himself both the president and the prime minister.

Throughout the 1970s, Marcos and his family gathered wealth and power. Many people believed he was misusing large sums of U.S. aid meant to help the Philippine people. He was living a life of luxury with his wife, Imelda, in the presidential palace, isolated from the people and protected by the military under his command. Imelda Marcos became ridiculed around the world for spending money on thousands of pairs of shoes while many Filipinos went barefoot and hungry.

Martial law lasted until 1981. That year, a majority of Filipinos approved of Marcos's virtual dictatorship and elected him for a six-year term as president.

Growing Opposition

Marcos's chief rival and critic, Benigno S. Aquino Jr., was imprisoned for more than seven years during the Marcos regime. In 1980, he was allowed to fly to the United States for heart surgery. Upon his return three years later, he stepped off a plane at Manila's airport and was shot to death. Many people believed someone close to Marcos or in the government had ordered the assassination.

Opposition to Marcos's rule grew. In 1986, Aquino's widow, Corazon Aquino, ran against Marcos in a presidential

Opponents of Ferdinand Marcos became unified in their support of Corazon Aquino (at podium) in the 1986 election.

election. Marcos was declared the winner, but many people believed that the election results were wrong and fraudulent.

Thus began a series of peaceful demonstrations known as the People Power Revolution. Hundreds of thousands of Filipinos risked being shot by forming human barricades to face down Marcos's soldiers and tanks. Nuns and priests fell to their knees in front of the advancing soldiers. Soldiers retreated, not wanting to fire on them. Marcos was soon driven from power, and Corazon Aquino was sworn in as president. Fearing further bloodshed, the United States arranged for Marcos, his wife, and their family to be airlifted out of the country. Marcos died in Hawaii in 1989.

On February 24, 1986, Filipinos cheered at the news that Ferdinand Marcos had fled the country.

The Steel Butterfly

Imelda Marcos, the widow of former Philippine president Ferdinand Marcos, was a symbol of excess and corruption during her husband's time in power. She served in his government and spent money freely, especially on shoes, of which she had a collection of about three thousand. When she and her husband fled the country in 1986, she was forced to leave her shoes behind. Today, 765 pairs of them are in the Marikina Shoe Museum in Manila.

After her husband's death, Imelda Marcos returned to the Philippines. She ran for president twice, but lost both times. She did, however, win election to Congress. Because of her beauty and her ability to weather adversity, she is known as the Steel Butterfly.

Recent Times

Corazon Aquino became president in 1986, promising to return the country to a democracy. A new constitution granted many reforms and provided for presidential terms of six years. She inherited her country's staggering financial problems as well as continued opposition from Marcos supporters. She faced continued conflict with Moro separatists and communist rebels, as well as natural disasters such as the eruption of Mount Pinatubo and a major earthquake. According to the new constitution, she could not run for reelection.

In 1992, Fidel V. Ramos, Corazon Aquino's former secretary of national defense, became president. He helped improve the economy, and in 1996 achieved a peace agreement with some of the Moro separatists. The Philippine government

Joseph Estrada takes the oath of office as mayor of Manila in 2013. Prior to entering politics, Estrada had been a popular film actor.

and Moro groups agreed to stop fighting, and a Muslim self-governing region was established in the southern Philippines.

But the country continued to struggle in its search for stability. The next president, Joseph Estrada, was accused of corruption and was removed from office on charges of plunder, having illegally amassed tens of millions of dollars. Despite this, he was elected mayor of Manila in 2013, twelve years after having been forced from the presidency.

Estrada had been granted a pardon by his successor, Gloria Macapagal-Arroyo. She was a professor of economics and a former senator who became popular early in her presidency because she implemented a policy of "holiday economics." She adjusted holidays to create longer weekends in order to boost domestic tourism and allow Filipinos more time with their families. The nation's economy grew under her leadership, even during the 2008 worldwide financial crisis.

In 2010, Benigno and Corazon Aquino's son, Benigno Aquino III, was elected president. Like the leaders before him, he had to deal with natural disasters, such as Super Typhoon Haiyan, which struck in 2013, killing more than 6,100 people. Aquino continued peace talks with the Moro rebels and signed a peace agreement with them in 2014. He also began reforms to curb corruption in the government. As these changes take hold and the nation's economy continues to expand, many Filipinos are optimistic about the future.

President Benigno Aquino III hands out relief supplies following a typhoon in 2012.

CHAPTER 5

Governing the Republic

FILIPINOS STRUGGLED FOR INDEPENDENCE FOR FOUR centuries. They were ruled first by Spain, then by the United States, and then by Japan during World War II. The First Republic of the Philippines was declared in 1898, and the Philippines became fully independent in 1946.

The Philippines has had three constitutions in its history. The current one was ratified, or approved, in 1987. The government is divided into three branches: executive, legislative, and judicial.

Opposite: **A Philippine voter fills out a ballot during a presidential election. All citizens at least eighteen years old can vote in the Philippines.**

Executive Branch

The president is the head of the executive branch. Just like the U.S. president, the president of the Philippines is both the head of state and the head of government. This means that he or she has both a ceremonial role as the leader of the country and a practical role as the person directing government policy and action. The president is also the commander in chief of the armed forces of the Philippines. The president is elected

Malacañang Palace was built in 1750 as the summer home of a wealthy Spaniard.

by popular vote, serves for six years, and cannot be reelected. The current president of the Philippines, elected in 2010, is Benigno S. Aquino III, a member of the Liberal Party. The presidential offices are in Malacañang Palace in Manila.

In the Family Business

Benigno S. Aquino III became president of the Philippines in 2010. A member of the Liberal Party, he is a former senator, a member of the House of Representatives, and a fourth-generation Filipino politician. His great-grandfather and grandfather were congressmen, his father was a senator who was assassinated for being a political activist, and he is the son of former president Corazon Aquino. He was urged to run for president after the death of his mother in 2009. Highly respected by Filipinos and people abroad, in 2013 Aquino was named one of the 100 Most Influential People in the World by *Time* magazine.

The president appoints cabinet secretaries. They are advisers who run the various departments of the government, such as finance, justice, health, and agriculture. They also advise the president on policy.

The president is also assisted by a vice president, who is elected by popular vote. Unlike the president, the vice president can serve two six-year terms. If the president dies or leaves office for any reason, the vice president becomes president. The vice president is usually, though not always, a member of the president's cabinet.

Jejomar Binay became vice president in 2010. He had earlier worked as a lawyer and as the mayor of Makati City.

National Flag

The national flag of the Philippines has a band of royal blue on the top and scarlet red on the bottom. The blue symbolizes peace, truth, and justice, while the red stands for patriotism and valor. On the left side of the flag is a white triangle. In the center of the triangle is a golden yellow sun symbolizing unity, freedom, and democracy. The sun has eight primary rays, which represent the nation's first group of provinces that started the 1896 revolution against Spain. Near each point of the triangle is a five-pointed yellow star representing the country's three main regions—Luzon, Visayas, and Mindanao. The flag was first displayed in 1898.

The Legislative Branch

The legislative, or law-making, branch of the government is the Congress of the Philippines. As in the United States, it is made up of two bodies, the Senate (upper house) and the House of Representatives (lower house). The Senate meets in Pasay, while the House of Representatives meets in Quezon City. Both are part of Metro Manila.

Members of the House of Representatives are elected to three-year terms. They can serve no more than three terms in a row. The House of Representatives has more than two hundred members. There are two kinds of representatives. Some represent the various congressional districts around the country. Others represent particular sectors of society, such as indigenous groups or labor groups.

The Senate has twenty-four members. Senators are elected to six-year terms. Senators are elected at large. This means

National Government of the Philippines

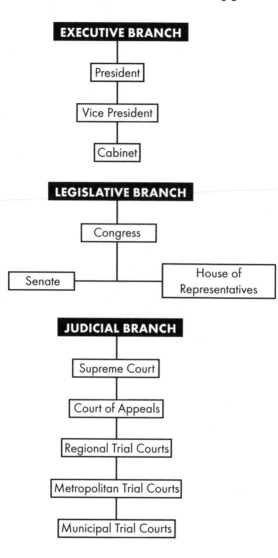

EXECUTIVE BRANCH

President

Vice President

Cabinet

LEGISLATIVE BRANCH

Congress

Senate

House of Representatives

JUDICIAL BRANCH

Supreme Court

Court of Appeals

Regional Trial Courts

Metropolitan Trial Courts

Municipal Trial Courts

that senators are not elected by people from a particular area. All the voters in the country vote for all the senators.

The Senate and House of Representatives have roughly equal powers. Every bill must be approved by both chambers

Loren Legarda is committed to helping the Philippines and making the world a better and safer place. She began her career as a journalist in the 1980s. She covered many major events, including the People Power Revolution, and she went on to host a television newscast. In 1998, she turned to politics, running for the Senate. She received the most votes of any of the candidates for Senate that year. She was elected again in 2007 and 2013.

As a senator, Legarda has focused on environmental issues. She has worked to pass laws limiting pollution and started a program that has planted millions of trees. She has also led the effort to deal with issues related to climate change. As sea levels rise and storms become more severe, her island nation will have to adapt.

before being sent to the president to be signed into law. If the president vetoes, or rejects, a bill, it can still become law if two-thirds of the people in both chambers pass it again.

Judicial Branch

The highest court in the Philippines is the Supreme Court. The Supreme Court of the Philippines has a chief justice and fourteen associate justices. Justices are appointed by the president on the recommendation of the Judicial and Bar Council. Justices may serve until age seventy. The Supreme Court meets in Manila.

Many trials are held in municipal or metropolitan trial courts. More serious crimes are tried in regional trial courts. The regional trial courts also hear appeals from the municipal and metropolitan trial courts. The Court of Appeals reviews decisions made in the regional trial courts. The Philippines also has a Court of Tax Appeals; the Sandiganbayan, which handles corruption cases; and Shari'a courts, which handle cases involving Islamic law.

Local Government

The country is divided into seventeen regions, each governed by a regional council. Regions are divided into more than seventy provinces, each with a governor, vice governor, and provincial board members. Each province includes a provincial capital city and several municipalities (towns). Elected mayors and councils govern the cities and municipalities.

Municipalities are composed of village committees called *barangays*, the smallest governing administrations in the nation. The name barangay comes from large oceangoing boats used by Malays for fishing and long-distance trade centuries ago. Each of the nation's forty-two thousand barangays has a captain, six council members, a treasurer, and a secretary. Every citizen is considered a member of a barangay assembly that meets to discuss national and local issues.

Regions

National Anthem

The national anthem of the Philippines is called "Lupang Hinirang" in Tagalog, which means "Chosen Land." The music was written in 1898 by Julian Felipe, and the lyrics were written a year later by José Palma, from his Spanish poem "Filipinas." It was adopted as the anthem of the revolutionary First Philippine Republic. During the American colonial period, singing the anthem in public was not permitted, but this changed in 1919. In 1938, the song was officially adopted as the Philippine national anthem.

Tagalog lyrics

Bayang magiliw,
Perlas ng Silanganan
Alab ng puso,
Sa Dibdib mo'y buhay.

Lupang Hinirang,
Duyan ka ng magiting,
Sa manlulupig,
Di ka pasisiil.

Sa dagat at bundok,
Sa simoy at sa langit mong bughaw,
May dilag ang tula,
At awit sa paglayang minamahal.

Ang kislap ng watawat mo'y
Tagumpay na nagniningning,
Ang bituin at araw niya,
Kailan pa ma'y di magdidilim,

Lupa ng araw ng luwalhati't pagsinta,
Buhay ay langit sa piling mo,
Aming ligaya na pag may mang-aapi,
Ang mamatay ng dahil sa iyo.

English translation

Beloved country,
Pearl of the Orient,
The heart's fervor,
In your chest is ever alive.

Chosen Land,
You are the cradle of the brave.
To the conquerors,
You shall never win.

Through the seas and mountains,
Through the air and your blue sky,
There is splendor in the poem and song
For beloved freedom.

The sparkle of your flag
Is shining victoriously.
Its stars and the sun
Shall forever never dim.

Land of the sun, of glory, and our affections,
Life is heaven in your arms.
It is our pleasure, when there are oppressors,
To die for you.

Party Politics

There are often up to a dozen political parties in the Philippines. Major parties include the Liberal Party, the United Nationalist Alliance, the Nationalist Party, and the Nationalist People's Coalition. Filipino citizens who are at least eighteen years old may vote.

While Filipinos cherish the idea of democracy, they also believe in strong family and cultural ties, so politicians are often elected because of family, cultural, ethnic, and other influences.

Several political parties joined into a coalition called Team PNoy in 2013. Senator Juan Edgardo "Sonny" Angara (center) campaigned under the PNoy banner.

Manila: A Closer Look

The city of Manila is the capital of the Philippines. With a population of more than 1.6 million in 2010, it is the second-largest city in the Philippines after Quezon City. Manila is the most densely populated city in the world. This means its people are packed into a relatively small area. More than 111,000 people live in every square mile of Manila. This is about four times the population density of New York City.

Manila is the center of a region called Metropolitan Manila, which includes sixteen neighboring cities, including Quezon City. The total population of Metro Manila, as the area is commonly called, is about 12 million, and the entire metropolitan area is home to about 25 million people. This thriving region is home to about one out of every four Filipinos.

People have been living in the Manila area for thousands of years. By the 1500s, Manila was a walled city under Muslim control. The city of Manila controlled trade on the Pasig River, which runs through the center of the city. In 1571, Spanish forces under Miguel López de Legazpi sailed into the river. The Spaniards attacked the city and took control of it. They chose the site to establish their colonial capital. Over the decades, Manila expanded and became the cultural and commercial heart of the Philippine islands.

Manila was at the center of the movement for Philippine independence in late 1800s. The Philippines was nearing independence when World War II began.

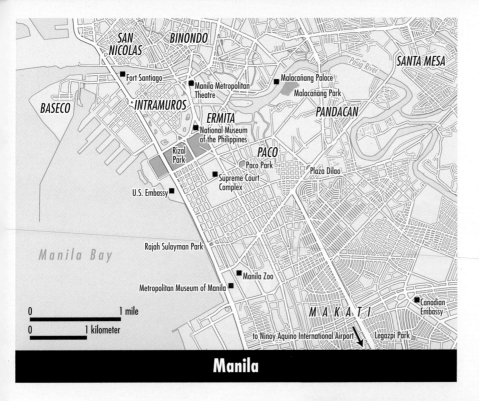

Manila

economy. It is home to the nation's main seaport. Manufacturing thrives in the city, with the production of clothing, chemicals, electronics, and much more. Food processing is also a major industry in the city.

More than a million tourists travel to Manila each year. Major attractions include the walled city of Intramuros, the National Museum of the Philippines (below), and Chinatown in the Binondo neighborhood. Major events in Manila are the Feast of the Black Nazarene and free concerts in Rizal Park. The city's nightclubs and shopping malls are also popular destinations.

The fight for control of Manila near the end of the war left the city in ruins. More than one hundred thousand civilian Filipinos were killed in the battle.

In the aftermath of the war, with the city devastated, the Philippine capital was move to Quezon City. Manila again became the seat of government in 1976. Today, the executive and judicial branches of the national government are centered in Manila. The Philippine Senate and House of Representatives are in other parts of Metro Manila.

Manila, the busy heart of the Philippines, is the national center for arts, education, entertainment, finance, media, and tourism. Manila has a diverse

CHAPTER 6

Making a Living

T HE PHILIPPINE ECONOMY IS ONE OF THE STRONGEST in East Asia. Its future looks bright, despite worldwide economic setbacks in the 1990s and early 2000s. In 2013, the nation's economy grew a robust 7.3 percent, one of the highest rates in Asia.

The nation's economy originally depended on agricultural trade. In recent years, the economy has become diversified, with industry, mining, and tourism all playing large roles.

Opposite: **A farmer works in a rice field in front of Mayon Volcano. In 2012, the Philippines was the world's eighth-largest rice producer.**

Agriculture

About one-third of the country's land is suitable for farming, and about one-third of Filipinos work in agriculture. Most of the food consumed in the Philippines is grown there.

Rice and corn grow on about two-thirds of the cultivated land in the islands. Rice is grown on flat terraces. These carved shelves of land are built to hold water. A whole family will work together to plant, harvest, and then sell the rice at roadside stands.

Pesos and Dollars

The official currency of the Philippines is the Philippine peso, which is made up of 100 centavos. Coins come in values of 1, 5, 10, and 25 centavos, and 1, 5, and 10 pesos. Coins worth less than 1 peso are rarely used. Paper money comes in values of 20, 50, 100, 200, 500, and 1,000 pesos.

Each denomination has a different dominant color, with images of important political figures on the front and natural wonders on the back. For example, the 20-peso note is orange. The front depicts Manuel Quezon, the first president of the commonwealth of the Philippines. The back shows a palm civet and the Banaue rice terraces.

In 2014, 1 Philippine peso equaled US$0.02, and US$1.00 equaled 45 Philippine pesos.

Weights and Measures

The Philippines uses the metric system. Under this system, the basic unit of length is the meter, which equals about 39 inches. Weight is measured in grams and kilograms. One kilogram equals about 2.2 pounds.

Other main crops are sweet potatoes and cassava, a starchy root. Bananas, pineapples, coconuts, mangoes, and sugarcane are grown for local use and for export. Farmers also raise hogs, chickens, and turkeys. People use the eggs themselves or sell them at local markets.

The main agricultural export is sugar, followed by coconut products. The Philippines produces 20 percent of the world's coconuts and exports many coconut products, such as shredded coconut and coconut oil. Coconut oil is used to make margarine, soap, plastics, candy, and cake frostings.

About half of the country's banana crop is exported, most of it to Japan. A third of the pineapples grown in the Philippines are consumed on the islands. The rest is shipped to other countries.

Fishing

Although thousands of species of fish are found in the waters in and around the Philippines, the nation's fishing industry remains relatively undeveloped. Most fish are caught for personal consumption or to be sold in markets, and large quantities of fish are imported.

Fish is the primary source of protein in the Filipino diet. Common fish caught and eaten in the Philippines are sardines, round scad, frigate tuna, anchovies, milkfish, and tilapia. People also catch mackerel, tuna, sea bass, red snapper, mullet, kawakawa, squid, and prawns.

A fisher tosses a net into Laguna del Bay.

What the Philippines Grows, Makes, and Mines

AGRICULTURE (2013)

Sugarcane	30,000,000 metric tons
Rice	25,000,000 metric tons
Coconuts	20,000,000 metric tons

MANUFACTURING (2013)

Food products	200,000,000,000 pesos
Petroleum and coal products	40,000,000,000 pesos
Chemicals	40,000,000,000 pesos

MINING (2013)

Coal	1,250,000 metric tons
Nickel ore	40,000 metric tons
Copper concentrate	225,000 metric tons

Mining and Manufacturing

The Philippines is home to an immense wealth of natural resources, with large deposits of gold, silver, iron ore, copper, chromate, and zinc. Most of these minerals are found on the islands of Luzon and Mindanao. Other resources mined in the Philippines include coal, limestone, manganese, and nickel.

Mining is on the rise in the Philippines. More than 1,200 areas were opened to mining exploration in 2013. Mining exports are expected to grow 13 percent and reach US$7.5 billion dollars by 2017.

Most manufacturing in the Philippines is concentrated in areas near Metro Manila. Factories produce cement, electronics, automobile parts, chemicals, petroleum products, clothing, foods and beverages, sugar, textiles, electronics, and wood products.

Services

Service industries make up the largest part of the Philippine economy. In 2013, it accounted for about 57 percent of the gross domestic product (GDP), the total value of all goods and services produced in the country.

In service industries, people provide a service for other people rather than making or growing something. People who work in hotels, restaurants, stores, and banks are employed in service industries. So are teachers, doctors, government workers, and auto mechanics. In the Philippines, many people involved in services work in trade.

Tourism, a major service industry, has been growing steadily in the Philippines. In 2013, nearly 4.7 million tourists arrived in the Philippines. Most came from the United States, Korea, and Japan. People travel to the Philippines to enjoy the beautiful beaches and mountains and explore historic sites in cities such as Manila and Cebu.

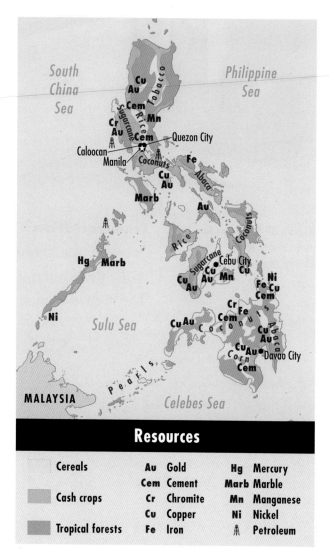

Resources

Cereals		Au	Gold	Hg	Mercury
		Cem	Cement	Marb	Marble
Cash crops		Cr	Chromite	Mn	Manganese
		Cu	Copper	Ni	Nickel
Tropical forests		Fe	Iron	⛏	Petroleum

Riders fill a commuter
train that serves
Metro Manila.

Transportation

Between the thousands of islands and the towering mountains, the Philippines can be a difficult place to get around. The nation has more than 130,000 miles (210,000 km) of

On the Beach

The Philippines is renowned for its spectacular white sand beaches. Some of the best Philippine beaches are found on the island of Boracay, in the central Visayas. Visitors swim and surf, snorkel and scuba dive. More tourists go cliff diving or explore distant caves. Boracay's combination of pristine beaches and excellent restaurants and resorts have made it one of the most popular tourist destinations in the Philippines.

Colorful Ride

The most colorful ways to get around in the Philippines is to ride in a jeepney. Jeepneys are small, brightly painted buses. Their name comes from the old U.S. military jeeps that the buses were originally made from. Jeepneys have established routes. When a passenger wants to get off, he or she taps on the ceiling or says *para*, "stop." Jeepneys can carry about eighteen passengers, but when they're packed, people sometimes climb on the roof. Jeepneys are among the cheapest and most common forms of transportation in the country. It is estimated that fifty thousand of them roll around Manila each day.

roads, but only about one-quarter of that length is paved. Most of the paved roads are in the Metro Manila area, but the number of paved roads in other areas is increasing.

The Philippines has a low rate of car ownership. Less than 5 percent of the people own cars. Instead, people often take buses. Manila also has a light rail system.

The largest airport in the country is the Ninoy Aquino International Airport, which serves Metro Manila. In 2012, more than 31 million passengers used the airport. Other important airports include Clark International Airport, which also serves Metro Manila, and Mactan-Cebu International Airport in the Visayas region.

Ports are crucial in the Philippines, as people travel from island to island on ferries or over bridges. Manila is the site of the nation's largest port. Cebu, Iloilo, and Davao are also major ports.

CHAPTER 7

Living and Learning

ABOUT HALF OF THE PEOPLE IN THE PHILIPPINES live in urban areas, and a quarter of them live in the area around Metro Manila. Philippine cities are often crowded, noisy, and polluted. The other half of the Philippine population lives in villages and towns along the coast or inland. In rural areas, Filipino homes may be made of wood with roofs of palm leaves. They are built on tall, strong poles so they are kept safe during the rainy season and floods.

Opposite: **An Ifugao man puts a roof on a traditional house in Luzon.**

Ethnic Groups

The Philippines is an ethnically diverse country. The people living there represent about one hundred different ethnic groups, some of who are descended from Malay people who probably migrated to the Philippine archipelago thousands of years ago.

The two largest ethnic groups in the country are the Tagalogs and the Cebuano Visayans. Most Tagalogs live in

Population of Largest Cities (2010 est.)	
Quezon City	2,761,720
Manila	1,652,171
Caloocan	1,489,040
Davao City	1,449,296
Cebu City	866,171

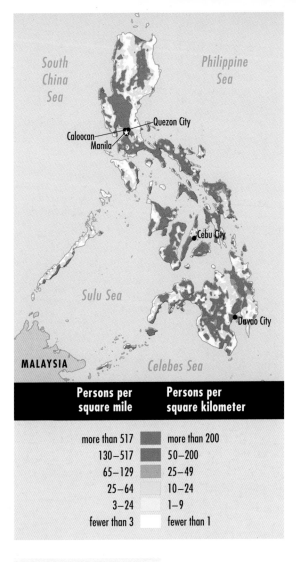

Persons per square mile	Persons per square kilometer
more than 517	more than 200
130–517	50–200
65–129	25–49
25–64	10–24
3–24	1–9
fewer than 3	fewer than 1

Filipino Ethnic Groups

Tagalog	28.1%
Cebuano	13.1%
Ilocano	9%
Bisaya	7.6%
Hiligaynon (Ilonggo)	7.5%
Bicol	6%
Waray	3.4%
Other	25.3%

the Metro Manila area and in the nearby provinces of Laguna, Bulacan, Batangas, and Cavite. Visayan groups live primarily in the central part of the country, such as in the islands of Cebu, Iloilo, Samar, and Leyte. Muslim Filipinos, called Moros, live in southern and western Mindanao and the Sulu islands. Tausugs, Yakans, and Samals live by the sea, while Maguindanaos and Maranaos live in central plains and mountainous regions of Lanao and Cotabato.

The Philippines is also home to some people who are not of Philippine ancestry. People of Chinese descent make up the largest group, an estimated 1.3 percent of the population. There are also small numbers of Americans, Arabs, Indians, Japanese, and others who live there.

Filipinos Around the World

Besides the more than one hundred million Filipinos living in the Philippines itself, another ten million Filipinos live in other countries. Many moved abroad temporarily to find work, while others moved away permanently.

More than three million Filipinos live in the United States. This is the largest number of Filipinos who live abroad. There are also large numbers of Filipinos in Saudi Arabia, Canada, and the United Arab Emirates.

A Filipino American man and his daughter attend the Philippine Independence Day Parade in New York City.

Ivatan

South China Sea

Philippine Sea

Ilocano
Igorot
Ifugao
Pangasinan
Kapampangan
Tagalog
Bicol
Waray
Hiligaynon
Bisaya
Cuyonon
V i s a y a s
Cebuano
Bisaya
Bisaya
Sulu Sea
Zamboangueño
Maranao
Cebuano
Maguindanao
Yakan
Hiligaynon
Tausug
M o r o
Samal
Celebes Sea

Ethnic Groups

Bicol	Ivatan	Tagalog
Ifugao	Kapampangan	Visayan groups
Igorot	Moro groups	Zamboangueño
Ilocano	Pangasinan	

Education

Filipino children are required to attend six years of elementary school. Elementary school starts at age seven and ends when children are thirteen. The students learn reading, writing, arithmetic, history, science, and other subjects, just like children in most other parts of the world.

Some Filipino boys and girls go to work after graduating from elementary school. Teenagers in the cities work in private companies, government agencies, or family-owned businesses such as restaurants or shops. Those in rural areas may work on a family farm.

Many other teenagers continue on to secondary school, which lasts four years. Many of the secondary schools are run by

Students take a trip to Rizal Park in Manila.

Women text in Metro Manila. Most people in the capital region speak Tagalog.

the Catholic Church. After completing secondary school, students may go on to study at one of about one thousand colleges and universities in the Philippines. Between 50 and 60 percent of Philippine teenagers go on to college or university. Filipinos are among the most highly educated people in the world.

Language

Filipinos speak many indigenous, or native, languages. Tagalog, used mainly in Manila and central Luzon, is the language of about 25 percent of Filipinos. Cebuano, which is spoken in Cebu and other parts of the central Philippines, is spoken by about 20 percent of the people.

The Philippines has two official languages, English and Filipino, which is a standardized form of Tagalog. Tagalog was

All Filipino children learn English in school.

chosen to be the common language of the Philippines in the 1930s. Boys and girls learn both English and Filipino in school. Half of all Filipinos speak, read, and write in both languages. Few Filipinos speak English as their first language. Instead, it is the language of business, government, and science.

Filipino children learn to speak whatever language their parents speak. In the early years of school, children are taught primarily in their native language. They begin learning Tagalog and English in second grade or later. In high school, however, most classes are in Tagalog or English.

The Spanish introduced the Latin alphabet, the alphabet in which English and Spanish are written, into the Philippines during the colonial era. Prior to that, Tagalog was written in an alphabet called Baybayin, which is related to writing sys-

Common Filipino Phrases

Magandang umaga po	Good morning
Magandang gabi po	Good evening
Oo	Yes
Hindi/hindi po	No
Salamat po	Thank you
Kumusta ka?	How are you?
Mabuhay	Hello/welcome
Paki	Please
Sige	Okay

tems used in India. Today, Tagalog uses a twenty-eight-letter version of the Latin alphabet. It includes the twenty-six letters that appear in English, plus ñ and *ng*.

Most newspapers in the Philippines are written in either English or Filipino.

CHAPTER 8

Spiritual Life

RELIGION IS IMPORTANT IN THE DAILY LIVES OF Filipinos. In the Philippines, early folk beliefs often meld with Christian and Islamic practices.

Most Filipinos are Roman Catholics. A smaller number belong to other Christian faiths or are Muslim.

Roman Catholics

Catholicism came to the Philippines with the arrival of missionaries from Spain in the 1500s. Today, more than 80 percent of Filipinos are Catholics. Most Philippine Catholics attend church regularly. In a 2013 survey, 37 percent of Filipino Catholics said they attend church every week, while 84 percent said they attend at least once a month.

Christmas is celebrated in a blend of Spanish, Philippine, and American customs. For nine days before Christmas Day, people attend early morning Mass. Worshippers hang elaborate lanterns and other decorations in their homes and join relatives and friends in caroling.

Opposite: **Filipinos light candles at a church in Cebu City.**

Religion in the Philippines	
Roman Catholic	80.9%
Evangelical	2.8%
Iglesia ni Cristo	2.3%
Philippine Independent Church (Aglipayan)	2%
Other Christian	4.5%
Muslim	5%
Other	1.8%
Unspecified	0.6%
None	0.1%

On Christmas Eve, people attend midnight Mass. Afterward, they return home for a large family meal. The remaining days of the Christmas season are spent visiting relatives or receiving guests in their homes. Children are especially urged to visit godparents.

Christmas lanterns are made for the holiday's celebrations. Children carry them in Christmas parades. The lanterns are made out of bamboo plant stems for the frames, which are then covered with colored paper. A light is placed inside each lantern.

The last week before Easter, which according to Christians is when Jesus rose from the dead, is a special time in the Philippines. As in the Spanish tradition, this is a time for

Markets sell lanterns and other colorful decorations during the Christmas season.

Remembering Ancestors

Filipino families celebrate All Saints' Day every year on November 1. In the days leading up to the holiday, they spruce up the graves of loved ones. Then, on the holiday itself, they spend much of the day and evening visiting their ancestors' graves. They honor their departed relatives by feasting and offering prayers.

Christian Filipinos to reflect on what they believe was Jesus's sacrifice for their souls. Most communities do a reading of the Passion of Christ, which is the story of the Last Supper and the trial and execution of Jesus. In Tagalog, this reading is called the *pabasa*. There are also many performances of the Passion Play called *sinakulo*.

A man plays the part of Jesus in a Passion Play in the Philippines.

Religious Holidays

Maundy Thursday	March or April
Good Friday	March or April
Easter Sunday	March or April
All Saints' Day	November 1
Christmas Day	December 25

Other Christians

All together, about 11.5 percent of Filipinos belong to Christian churches other than the Roman Catholic Church. The Philippine Independent Church is the most similar to Catholicism in the way its members worship. It was founded in 1902, in the aftermath of the Philippine Revolution. Its members broke away from the Catholic Church because they believed Spanish priests retained too much influence in the church and mistreated Filipinos. The break was led by a former priest named Gregorio Aglipay y Labayán, so the new church's members are sometimes called Aglipayans. Today, the Philippine Independent Church has a close association with the Church of England, which in the United States is called the Episcopal Church. About 2 percent of Filipinos are Aglipayans.

Another church that started in the Philippines is Iglesia ni Cristo. It was founded in 1914 by Felix Manalo, who became the executive minister of the church. He was succeeded first by his son and then by his grandson, Eduardo, who remains in charge of the church today. The Iglesia ni Cristo is centered at the Central Temple in Quezon City. The current building, a towering church that can hold seven thousand people, was completed in 1984. The church takes a literal interpretation of the Bible.

Today, the Iglesia ni Cristo has about two million members in the Philippines, and many more millions around the world.

A smaller number of Filipinos belong to other Christian churches. These include the United Church of Christ, the Church of Jesus Christ of Latter-day Saints (Mormon church), Jehovah's Witnesses, and the United Pentecostal Church. Many of the Protestant churches came to the islands during the years when the United States controlled the islands.

Worshippers leave the main church of the Iglesia ni Cristo. Its members believe its founder, Felix Manalo, was God's final prophet, or messenger.

Traditional Beliefs

Before the arrival of Islam and Christianity in the Philippines, people practiced animism, the belief that all plants, animals, and objects have their own spirit. Some Filipinos also believed in a universal god, Bathala, who ruled the universe and decided their fate.

Today, some Filipinos mix Christianity and these ancient beliefs. They might pray to the rain god during a drought, or the earth god for a bountiful harvest. They also pray to their ancestors for protection and guidance. This practice is sometimes called split-Christianity.

Filipino Muslims rally in support of a peace agreement between the Philippine government and a Muslim separatist movement in the southern part of the country.

Other Faiths

Islam came to the Philippines in the 1300s and had become common in the islands as far north as Manila by the time the Spaniards arrived in the sixteenth century. After the Spaniards took control of the islands, Roman Catholicism

spread quickly and Islam became less common. Today, about 5 percent of Filipinos are Muslim. They are known as Moros. Most live in the southern part of the country, in the Mindanao island group.

Filipinos pray in a park in Manila during a celebration of the end of Ramadan.

Like Muslims around the world, Filipino Muslims fast during the daylight hours of Ramadan, the ninth and holiest month of the Muslim calendar. They fast to improve self-discipline, purify their hearts, and feel a greater connection to the poor. At the end of the month, they celebrate 'Id al-Fitr, also called Hari Raya Poasa in the Philippines. For this holiday, they put on their best clothes and enjoy lavish feasts.

The Philippines is also home to a small number of Hindus, Buddhists, and Baha'is.

CHAPTER 9

Culture, Arts, and Sports

PHILIPPINE CULTURE IS A MIXTURE OF ASIAN AND Western traditions. Some art forms and sports developed in the Philippines and date back thousands of years, while others are quite modern. But whether they are old or new, native Filipino or Spanish, they all speak to the Philippine spirit.

Opposite: **Filipinos have been weaving fabric in traditional patterns for hundreds of years.**

Art

Many Filipinos are skilled in traditional crafts such as basket weaving and mat making. Another traditional craft is weaving fabrics from pineapple and banana fibers. Some of these fabrics are finely embroidered. Other crafts include carving animals, birds, and other objects from wood, as well as furniture making.

Pottery making dates back thousands of years in the Philippines. Early Filipinos painted on some of the pots they made. After Europeans arrived in the islands, some Filipinos began painting using Spanish techniques and themes. Painters such as Juan Luna, who was active in the nineteenth century, worked in the Spanish style and created works that depicted religious, political, or historic themes. Others, such as the twentieth-century painter Victorio C. Edades, worked in a more modern and individual style. Contemporary painters exhibit their work at many private galleries and at the Metropolitan Museum of Manila. Native Philippine arts and crafts also are on display there.

A Filipino artist paints scenes from Palawan Island.

Actors take part in a play about José Rizal in Rizal Park in Manila.

Drama

The Philippines has a strong tradition of drama. Many performances depict the history and religious traditions of the nation. Some of these involve a type of Spanish performance called a *zarzuela*, which alternates between people speaking and singing as they tell a story. In some rural areas, popular zarzuela performances depict conflict between Christians and Moros during the Spanish colonial years. Western plays are performed at universities and by professional theater groups in major cities.

Children are active in their country's theater life. Many children who want to act hope to perform in the Repertory

Philippines Children's Theatre, which stages classics and modern plays and musicals.

Dance

Filipinos love to dance, at home, in parks, at discos, and in ballrooms. They also love to watch dance performances at festivals and in theaters. Styles range from folk dances to clas-

Dancing Traditions

A favorite folk dance in the Philippines is called the *singkil*. A girl dances between moving bamboo sticks held at ground level. In another folk dance, the *tinikling*, the dancer mimics the movements of the tikling bird, a heron, as it walks through tall grasses. In the *binasuan*, dancers balance three glasses of liquid—one on each hand and one on the head—while they gracefully dance.

Lisa Macuja-Elizalde is the artistic director of Ballet Manila as well as a dancer with the company.

sical ballet to ballroom dancing, which became a craze in the 1980s. The most famous folk dance company is the Bayanihan Dance Company, which was founded in the late 1950s.

Patriotic themes dominated dance at the 1998 Centennial Celebration of Philippine Independence. Choreographer Agnes Locsin created a ballet called *La Revolucion Filipina* for the country's most famous ballet company, Ballet Philippines.

Lea Salonga is one of the best-selling Filipino singers of all time.

Lisa Macuja-Elizalde, the most celebrated prima ballerina, performs with the Ballet Manila. She was the first foreign soloist to join the Russian Kirov Ballet, in 1984.

Music

Many Filipinos learn to play musical instruments at home or in school and perform as amateurs at festivals or music concerts. The most popular instrument is the guitar. Professional singers and musicians perform folk, jazz, and rock and roll at clubs in cities and towns. One Filipino singer who has achieved worldwide fame is Lea Salonga. She played the lead in the original production of the musical *Miss Saigon*, winning theater's highest honors: a Tony Award for her performance in New York City and an Olivier Award for her performance in London, England.

Singing contests have long been popular in the Philippines. In recent years, as TV shows such as *Philippine Idol* and *The Voice of the Philippines* have been produced, they have become even more common.

Charice Pempengco began appearing on TV singing competitions as a child and soon gained an international reputation via her YouTube videos. She later joined the cast of the TV show *Glee* and became the first Asian solo act to have an album reach the top ten on the *Billboard* charts.

Classical music is performed at schools and universities. The Philippine Philharmonic Orchestra performs at the Manila Metropolitan Theater. Teenage classical musicians often win scholarships to study music abroad. Some classical performers have gone on to perform around the world. For example, opera star Jovita Fuentes made her stage debut in Milan, Italy, in 1924. She later helped popularize opera in the Philippines.

Women play a kulintang. This instrument can include between five and nine gongs.

Traditional Philippine music is played at festivals in villages and tribal communities. Instruments include gongs called *kulintang*, the bamboo guitar, a bamboo nose flute (played through the nose rather than the mouth), and a type of mouth harp called the *kubing*.

Literature

The literary tradition in the Philippines began in the late 1800s with the independence movement when Filipinos began writing patriotic pamphlets and books. Most famous was José Rizal's 1886 novel, *Noli Me Tangere* (*Touch Me Not*), which exposed Spanish cruelty and explored Filipino dreams of freedom. Rizal also wrote other popular novels, including *El Filibusterismo* (*The Subversive*).

Filipinos began writing stories and books in English during the American colonization, again boldly writing to encourage nationalism and exposing social problems. In recent years, novels and nonfiction books by Filipino authors have covered a wide range of subjects, but many continue to reflect on historic themes and the long struggle for independence. For example, Nick Joaquin's writings include *Cave and Shadows*, a novel that takes place during the martial law of the Marcos era, as well as a biography of Benigno Aquino and many other works.

Comic books are as popular in the Philippines as they are in the United States. Stores and outdoor stands that sell comic books are favorite hangouts for young people.

Fans gather around a table to pick up comic books during Free Comic Day at a bookstore in Metro Manila.

Movies

Philippine movie theaters mainly show popular new American films. In recent years, more Filipino-made films have also been shown. Most are either romances or dramas that sometimes have serious themes about political or social conditions. In recent years, movies such as *Small Voices* (2002), *Service* (2008), and *Butchered* (2009) have received international acclaim.

The film *Small Voices* concerns a teacher at a troubled school who engages the children by getting them involved in a singing contest.

Over his career, Manny Pacquiao has won world championships in eight different weight classes. They ranged from flyweight, up to 112 pounds (51 kg), to super welterweight, up to 154 pounds (70 kg).

Sports

Basketball is a national passion in the Philippines. Basketball courts are found in nearly every town plaza and neighborhood in small villages and large cities. Americans introduced basketball to the Philippines during the colonial era. The Philippine Basketball Association (PBA) began in 1975, making it the oldest professional basketball league in Asia. In fact, it is the oldest in the world outside the United States.

Golf, volleyball, badminton, karate, tennis, and boxing are also popular in the Philippines. The most famous Filipino athlete is Emmanuel "Manny" Pacquiao, a boxer who is also a member of the House of Representatives. Pacquiao has won ten world titles and was named "Fighter of the Decade" for the 2000s by the Boxing Writers Association of America.

Many Filipinos enjoy watching and playing jai alai, a sport played on a court with three walls. Each player has a wicker basket, called a *cesta*, tied to one arm. One player hurls a hard rubber ball from the cesta against a wall. The opponent must catch the ball in his cesta before it bounces more than once and then hurl it back against the wall for the other player to catch. In this wickedly fast game, balls sometimes fly at speeds of more than 180 miles per hour (290 kph).

Cockfighting, which is banned in some countries, is very popular in the Philippines. Many towns have a cockpit. Crowds of people gather on Sundays and holidays to watch and bet on fights between two roosters.

Each year, athletes compete in the Philippine National Games, like a national Olympics. Events include gymnastics, running, swimming, volleyball, and polo. Polo players ride horses and use sticks to hit balls into goals.

Games People Play

A favorite sport among Philippine boys is a form of martial arts called *arnis*. Players use long sticks to throw each other off balance.

Girls and boys alike play *sipa*, which is something like volleyball. Players stand on either side of a net and hit a ball over it. But they can use only their knees and feet to hit the ball. It isn't easy, but it is fun.

Many young people also enjoy flying kites.

CHAPTER 10

Philippine Ways

FILIPINOS COME FROM VARIED CULTURES, BUT THEY have many things in common. One of the strongest is family closeness. Filipinos live in the same house as their extended family members or near them. This may include parents, brothers, sisters, aunts, uncles, cousins, and grandparents. Most boys share bedrooms with their brothers, and girls share bedrooms with their sisters.

Filipino families live in clans led by a godfather (*compadre*) and a godmother (*comadre*). These figures are community leaders who may not be blood relatives but become part of the family by helping them in good and bad times. The godparents find clan members jobs, help settle disputes, and arrange funerals.

Another trait common to Filipinos is gratitude. They never forget even a small favor, and they always repay it, if possible. One form of repayment is for family members to vote for their godfather or godmother in elections.

Opposite: **A Philippine family takes a ride on a motorcycle. The average family in the Philippines has three children.**

Children play on a peaceful street on the island of Marinduque, south of Luzon.

City and Country

City life and rural life differ greatly in the Philippines. Daily life in the cities is very similar to that in the United States and Canada today. Young Filipinos in cities live in apartments or small houses similar to those in North America. Social life in the cities is varied and plentiful. Young people can attend concerts and dances. They can go to sporting events at schools and at public stadiums.

Life in Filipino villages and rural areas, on the other hand, is in some ways more like rural life in years past in North America. Some families live in small houses built on wooden stilts to protect them from floods. Boys and girls work in family fields after school and may ride a water buffalo home at dusk for dinner. There are some modern aspects to life in villages, however. After the evening meal children play games such as basketball. After dark, they do their school homework or work on a computer. Even remote villages have televisions, cell phones, and computers.

Good Food

Philippine cuisine consists of Southeast Asian food and ingredients with many Spanish, American, and Chinese influences. Dishes often combine strong sweet, salty, and sour flavors.

Rice is the main food of Filipinos. It is often eaten with fish, chicken, or pork. Fruits such as bananas, mangoes, coconuts, and pineapples are often used in dishes. Common vegetables include cabbage, eggplants, and beans.

Adobo is the unofficial national dish of the Philippines. It is a sauce made with vinegar, soy sauce, and garlic. Meats and vegetables are often cooked in adobo sauce. Barbecued meats are popular, as are stews made with a mix of meat and vegetables, often in a tomato sauce or a peanut sauce base.

Fried bananas are popular snacks in the Philippines.

One popular dessert is *halo-halo*, which is made of dried fruit, custard, and crushed ice mixed together.

Most Filipinos eat three or four times a day. Breakfast is often the largest meal. Many Filipinos start the day with bread rolls, cheese, fried rice, eggs, and meat or fish. They wash it down with strong coffee. Lunch tends to be rice and a main dish such as adobo. Many Filipinos have an afternoon snack called *merienda*. This often consists of coffee and sweet pastries or savory pastries filled with meat. It can also include street foods such as rice cakes or a banana or sweet potato on a stick. Fish is commonly served at dinner.

A family enjoys a meal outdoors.

Chicken Adobo

Adobo sauce is simple to make and keeps for several days. Have an adult help you with this recipe.

Ingredients

½ cup white vinegar	1 tablespoon black peppercorns
½ cup soy sauce	3 bay leaves
4 garlic cloves, crushed	4 chicken thighs

Directions

Combine the vinegar, soy sauce, garlic, peppercorns, and bay leaves in a large bowl. Put the chicken into the bowl and coat it with the sauce. Cover the bowl and refrigerate it for 1 to 3 hours. Put the chicken and sauce into a pot on the stove. Cover the pot and bring the sauce to a boil, and then lower the heat. Let the chicken simmer in the covered pot for about 30 minutes, stirring often. Then uncover the pot and simmer until the sauce is thick and the chicken is tender. Serve the chicken adobo with rice. Enjoy!

A bride walks down a church aisle during her wedding in Manila.

Marriage

Marriage ceremonies in the Philippines are influenced by Spanish, American, and indigenous Filipino traditions. In the era before the Spanish arrived, weddings lasted three days and were officiated by a *babaylan*, a priest or priestess. The couple went to the priest's house, and they were blessed as they held hands over a container of raw rice. After the ceremony, the couple received gifts.

Spaniards brought Catholic rituals to marriage ceremonies in the islands. Marriages became not only the union of a man and a woman, but a joining together of two families.

A typical marriage proposal is called *pamanhikan* in Tagalog. A would-be groom and his parents go to the house of the would-be bride and ask her parents for their consent. If the proposal is accepted, plans are made for the wedding regarding the date, the finances involved, and the list of guests. Wedding expenses are usually paid by the groom and his parents.

Most Filipino weddings are held in a church. The bride wears a white wedding gown and veil, while the groom wears black trousers and an untucked white, embroidered collarless shirt. After a bridal procession, the couple stands before the priest or minister, the bride holding a bouquet of flowers. Rings are exchanged. The groom then gives the bride thirteen gold or silver coins, representing a pledge to care for her and their future children.

Muslim weddings are often prearranged by families. A religious leader called an imam usually presides over the wedding ceremony.

It Is Said...

Some people in the Philippines have old superstitions about pregnancy. For instance, it is said that if a pregnant woman radiates beauty she will give birth to a son. If she craves sweets, the baby will be a girl. It is said that a pregnant woman should not attend a funeral because the spirit of the dead might possess the baby.

Filipinos carry a coffin on the way to a funeral.

Funeral Customs

Filipino funeral customs arise from a wide range of traditions. Most Filipinos believe in some form of a life after death. Catholic Filipinos often hold a wake honoring the person who has died, which lasts from three days to a week. In rural

Two New Years

Filipinos celebrate two New Year's holidays. January 1, as it is around the world, is the Philippine New Year. Filipinos also celebrate the Chinese New Year held in January or February. Both holidays are celebrated with parties and fireworks. Chinese New Year also includes parades with dragon dancers.

National Holidays

New Year's Day	January 1
Chinese New Year's Day	January or February
People Power Anniversary	February 25
Maundy Thursday	March or April
Good Friday	March or April
Holy Saturday	March or April
Day of Valor	April 9
Labor Day	May 1
Independence Day	June 12
Ninoy Aquino Day	August 21
National Heroes Day	Last Monday of August
All Saints' Day	November 1
Bonifacio Day	November 30
Christmas Eve	December 24
Christmas Day	December 25
Rizal Day	December 30
New Year's Eve	December 31

In addition, two Muslim holidays that change dates in the Western calendar from year to year are also national holidays.

'Id al-Fitr (End of Ramadan)

'Id al-Adha (Feast of the Sacrifice)

areas, wakes may be held in a home, while in cities they are held in funeral parlors. The family of the deceased person usually serves food and tea or coffee. Visitors gather outside the home or funeral parlor to talk, sing, listen to music, or play card games. These activities help the mourners stay awake on nightly vigils. Many mourners also pray for the person who has died. On the funeral day, a coffin carrying the deceased is taken by hearse to a church for a funeral Mass and then to a cemetery for burial.

Pakikisama

Mothers teach their children the custom of *pakikisama*, which is the idea of being united in a group. It implies being cooperative and considerate. Children learn at an early age to be kind and considerate to other people, especially their elders. They learn it is not polite to criticize, yell at, or bully other people.

Clothing

Filipinos dress casually in cotton clothes that help them stay cool in hot weather. Most boys wear jeans and T-shirts. Girls wear cotton skirts and tops. Men and women working in the cities might dress a little more formally. Men might wear black pants and a long embroidered shirt called a *barong tagalog*. Women might wear long skirts called *sayas*.

The barong tagalog developed from a simple shirt worn by people in the Philippines before the arrival of the Spaniards. It became popular as formal wear in the 1950s.

Friendly Filipinos

Perhaps the best-known and most visible trait of Filipinos is friendliness. For Filipinos, smiling is a way of talking. They don't need to say hello to anyone. They smile and raise their eyebrows to show they want to be friendly.

Filipinos practice a trait that they call *pakikisama* by showing a deep camaraderie and helpfulness toward people around them. If there is any way Filipinos can help their family and neighbors, they do it. Filipinos are also friendly and generous toward strangers. They are happy to talk to visitors. Strangers to a village are invited into people's homes and given food.

Filipinos tend to have a relaxed attitude toward life. A Tagalog term for it is *bahala na*, meaning "what happens, happens." The people of the Philippines work hard to make a good living, often believing that what happens is in the hands of God.

Children share an umbrella on a rainy day near Manila.

Philippine Hospitality

Filipinos have a reputation for being extremely generous toward strangers. Jean, a Filipino living in Metro Manila, recalls a time she was traveling in the countryside:

My husband and I found ourselves in a small village with no hotel room to rent for the night. When a Filipino couple learned of our problem, they invited us into their small home. They fed us rice and fish for dinner and offered us a bed to sleep on, with bedcovers freshly washed and pressed, and covered by a mosquito net. We didn't learn until the next morning that our hosts had given us the only bed in their house, and they had slept on the kitchen floor.

Timeline

Callao Man lives in the Philippine islands. — **ca. 60,000 years ago**

People in central Luzon build massive rice terraces. — **ca. 2,000 years ago**

Filipinos begin trading with China. — **ca. 900s CE**

Islam spreads to the Philippines. — **1400s**

Ferdinand Magellan leads the first European expedition to the Philippines. — **1521**

Miguel López de Legazpi establishes the first Spanish settlement in the Philippines, on the island of Cebu. — **1565**

Manila is established. — **1571**

The Spanish make education free for all Filipinos. — **1863**

ca. 2500 BCE — The Egyptians build the pyramids and the Sphinx in Giza.

ca. 563 BCE — The Buddha is born in India.

313 CE — The Roman emperor Constantine legalizes Christianity.

610 — The Prophet Muhammad begins preaching a new religion called Islam.

1054 — The Eastern (Orthodox) and Western (Roman Catholic) Churches break apart.

1095 — The Crusades begin.

1215 — King John seals the Magna Carta.

1300s — The Renaissance begins in Italy.

1347 — The plague sweeps through Europe.

1453 — Ottoman Turks capture Constantinople, conquering the Byzantine Empire.

1492 — Columbus arrives in North America.

1500s — Reformers break away from the Catholic Church, and Protestantism is born.

1776 — The U.S. Declaration of Independence is signed.

1789 — The French Revolution begins.

1865 — The American Civil War ends.

1879 — The first practical lightbulb is invented.

PHILIPPINE HISTORY

1892	The Katipunan, a secret independence group, is formed.
1898	The Spanish-American War begins; the Treaty of Paris ends the war and gives the Philippines to the United States.
1899	The Philippine-American War begins.
1902	The Philippine-American War ends.
1935	The Philippines gains commonwealth status.
1941	The Japanese attack the Philippines.
1942	Thousands of Philippine and American soldiers die during the Bataan Death March.
1946	The Philippines gains independence.
1954	Government forces defeat the Huk Rebellion.
1965	Ferdinand Marcos is elected president.
1972	Marcos declares martial law.
1983	Opposition leader Benigno Aquino Jr. is assassinated.
1986	Widespread protests force Marcos to leave the country; Corazon Aquino becomes president.
1991	Mount Pinatubo erupts, causing widespread destruction.
1996	A peace agreement ends fighting between government forces and some Muslim separatist groups in the south.
2013	Super Typhoon Haiyan strikes the islands, killing more than 6,100 people.

WORLD HISTORY

1914	World War I begins.
1917	The Bolshevik Revolution brings communism to Russia.
1929	A worldwide economic depression begins.
1939	World War II begins.
1945	World War II ends.
1969	Humans land on the Moon.
1975	The Vietnam War ends.
1989	The Berlin Wall is torn down as communism crumbles in Eastern Europe.
1991	The Soviet Union breaks into separate states.
2001	Terrorists attack the World Trade Center in New York City and the Pentagon near Washington, D.C.
2004	A tsunami in the Indian Ocean destroys coastlines in Africa, India, and Southeast Asia.
2008	The United States elects its first African American president.

Fast Facts

Official name: Republic of the Philippines

Capital: Manila

Official languages: Filipino and English

Manila

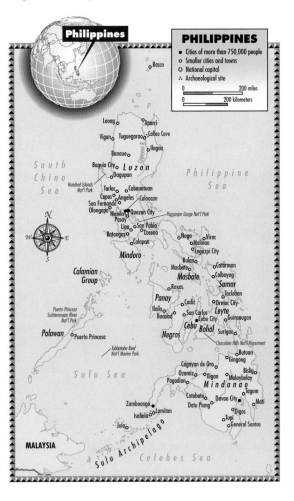

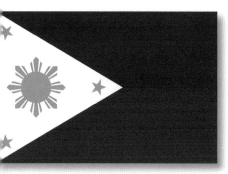

National flag

Palawan Islands

Official religion:	None
National anthem:	"Lupang Hinirang" ("Chosen Land")
Government:	Constitutional democracy
Head of state:	President
Head of government:	President
Area of country:	About 120,000 square miles (310,000 sq km)
Number of islands:	7,107
Highest elevation:	Mount Apo, 9,692 feet (2,954 m)
Lowest elevation:	Sea level along the coasts
Longest river:	Cagayan River, Luzon, 220 miles (354 km)
Largest lake:	Laguna de Bay, Luzon, 356 square miles (922 sq km)
Average high temperature:	In Manila, 86°F (30°C) in January, 94°F (34°C) in May
Average low temperature:	In Manila, 70°F (21°C) in January, 76°F (24°C) in June
Average annual rainfall:	35 to 216 inches (89 to 549 cm) per year

Chocolate Hills

Currency

National population (2013 est.):	98,734,798	

Population of major cities (2010 est.):

Quezon City	2,761,720
Manila	1,652,171
Caloocan	1,489,040
Davao City	1,449,296
Cebu City	866,171

Landmarks:
- ▶ *Banaue Rice Terraces*, Ifugao
- ▶ *Chocolate Hills*, Bohol Island
- ▶ *Fort Santiago*, Manila
- ▶ *Magellan's Cross*, Cebu City
- ▶ *National Museum of the Philippines*, Manila

Economy: In 2013, about one-third of Filipino workers were employed in farming. Major crops include rice, corn, sugarcane, coconuts, and pineapples. Food processing is a major manufacturing industry. Electronics, clothing, chemicals, and petroleum products are also made in the Philippines. Services make up the largest part of the economy. Many Filipinos work in the tourism industry and trade.

Currency: The Philippine peso. In 2014, 1 Philippine peso equaled US$0.02, and US$1.00 equaled 45 Philippine pesos.

System of weights and measures: Metric system

Literacy rate (2005 est.): 95%

Schoolchildren

Lea Salonga

Common Filipino words and phrases:

Magandang umaga po	Good morning
Magandang gabi po	Good evening
Oo	Yes
Hindi/hindi po	No
Salamat po	Thank you
Mabuhay	Hello/welcome
Paki	Please

Prominent Filipinos:

Emilio Aguinaldo (1869–1964)
Rebel leader and president

Andres Bonifacio (1863–1897)
Revolutionary leader

Juan Luna (1857–1899)
Painter

Lisa Macuja-Elizalde (1964–)
Ballerina

Ferdinand Marcos (1917–1989)
President and dictator

Emmanuel "Manny" Pacquiao (1978–)
Boxer and politician

José Rizal (1861–1896)
Writer and scientist

Lea Salonga (1971–)
Singer

To Find Out More

Books

▶ Burgan, Michael. *Philippines*. Chicago: Heinemann, 2012.

▶ Golay, Michael. *Spanish-American War*. New York: Chelsea House, 2010.

▶ Greenberger, Robert. *The Bataan Death March: World War II Prisoners in the Pacific*. Minneapolis: Compass Point Books, 2009.

Music

▶ *Music of the Philippines: Fiesta Filipina*. West Sussex, United Kingdom: ARC Music, 2003.

▶ Salonga, Lea. *The Journey So Far*. Los Angeles: LML Music, 2011.

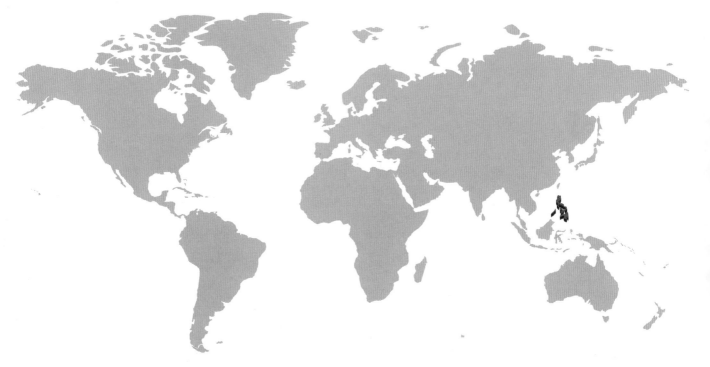

▶ Visit this Scholastic Web site for more information on the Philippines:
www.factsfornow.scholastic.com
Enter the keywords **The Philippines**

Index

Page numbers in *italics* indicate illustrations.

A

adobo (national dish), 119, 121, *121*
Aeta people, *42*, 43
Aglipay y Labayán, Gregorio, 98
agriculture
    bananas, 80
    children and, 90
    corn, 79
    crops, 79–80, 82
    early settlers, 44
    economy and, 79, 82
    farmland, 9, 20, *20*, 44, *44*
    forests and, 33
    government and, 58, 69
    Ifugao region, 44
    jobs in, 79, 90
    livestock, 37, *37*, 80, 118
    Luzon Island, *20*, 44
    Mount Pinatubo volcano, 29
    rice, 44, *78*, 79
    tenant farmers, 56
    terrace farming, 20, *20*, 44, *44*,
        79, 80
    trade and, 79, 80
Aguilar, Ferdinand "Freddie," 111
Aguinaldo, Emilio, 49, *50*, 133
Agusan River, 22
Albay province, 47
All Saints' Day, 97, *97*

Angara, Juan Edgardo "Sonny," 75
animal life
    animism, 100
    bats, 37
    birds, 39, *39*, 106, 115
    carabao, 37, *37*
    chevrotains, 35–36
    cockfighting, 115
    crafts and, 103
    livestock, 37, *37*, 80, 118
    mammals, 35–37
    tamaraws, 36
    tarsiers, 36, *36*
Aquino, Benigno S., Jr., 61, 112
Aquino, Benigno S., III, 27, 65, *65*,
    68, *68*
Aquino, Corazon, 61–62, *61*, 63, 68
archaeology, 43
arnis (martial art), 115, *115*
art, 103–104, *104*, 133
Ateneo de Manila University, 31

B

Baguio City, 24, 28, *28*, 30
Baha'i religion, 101
Ballet Manila, *107*, 108
Ballet Philippines, 107
basketball, 114
Bataan Death March, *54*, 55, *55*
Bataan Peninsula, 54, 55
Batangas province, 88
Bathala (god), 100
bats, 37
Bayanihan Dance Company, 107
"Bayan Ko" (Ferdinand "Freddie"
    Aguilar), 111
Baybayin alphabet, 92–93
beverages, 35
Binay, Jejomar, 69
Binondo neighborhood, 77
birds, 39, *39*, 106, 115
Bohol Island, 18, 20, *20*

Bonifacio, Andres, 31, 133
Boracay Island, 84
boxing, 114, *114*, 133
Buddhism, 101
Bulacan province, 88
buses, 85, *85*
Butchered (movie), 113
Butig Mountains, 19

C

Cabayugan River, 23
Cagayan River, 17, 22
Callao Cave, 43
Callao Man, *42*, 43
Caloocan, 31, 87
Camp O'Donnell, 55
Cano, Juan Sebastián del, 46, *46*
Capas, 55
capital cities. *See* Manila; Quezon City.
Caraballo Mountains, 19
carabao (water buffalo), 37, *37*
cars, 85
Casaroro Falls, *32*
Catholicism. *See* Roman Catholicism.
Cave and Shadows (Nick Joaquin), 112
Cavite province, 88
Cebuano Visayan people, 87
Cebu City, 31, 83, 85, 87, *94*
Cebu Island
    beaches, *41*
    Cebu City, 31, 87, *94*
    location of, 18
    Spanish colonization, 46
    Spanish exploration, 45, *45*
    Visayan people on, 88
Celebes Sea, 15
cell phones, 118
Central Visayas region, *32*
chevrotains, 35–36
children, 89–90, *89*, *90*, 92, *92*, 96,
    105–106, 115, *115*, *116*, 118, *118*,
    123, *123*, 126, *127*

Chinatown, 77
Chinese New Year, 124, *124*
Chinese people, 44
Chocolate Hills, 20, *20*
Christmas holiday, 95–96, *96*
Church of England, 98
Church of the Holy Child, 31
cities. *See also* Manila; Quezon City.
   Baguio City, 24, 28, *28*, 30
   Caloocan, 31, 87
   Cebu City, 31, 83, 85, 87, *94*
   Davao City, 31, 85, 87
   Iloilo City, 85
   Legazpi City, 47
   Makati City, 69
   Ormoc City, 26, *26*
   Pasay, 70
   San Fernando, 55
   Tacloban, 24
Clark International Airport, 85
classical music, 110
climate, 13, *13*, 17, 23, 24–26, *24*, 28,
   35, 65, *65*, 72, 87
clothing, 101, 123, 126, *126*
coastline, 8, 9, 16, *16*, 17, *17*, *19*, 21,
   21, *41*, 84, *84*
cockfighting, 115
coconut palm trees, 35, *35*
comic books, 112, *112*
communications, 72, *91*, 93, 118
communism, 56
Congress of the Philippines, 58, 70
constitutions, 59–60, 63, 67
Cordillera Central mountain chain, 19
Corregidor Island, 54
Cotabato region, 88
Court of Appeals, 73
crafts, *102*, 103
crops, 79–80, 82
Cruz de Uyanguren, José, 31
currency (Philippine peso), 41, 80, *80*

D
dance, 106–108, *106*, *107*, 133
Davao City, 31, 85, 87
Diwata Mountains, 19
drama, 105–106, *105*

E
earthquakes, 26, *27*, 28, 29, 30, 63
Easter holiday, 96–97
economy
   agriculture and, 79, 82
   currency (Philippine peso), 41,
     80, *80*
   Diosdado Macapagal and, 58
   diversity of, 79
   fishing industry, 81, *81*
   Gloria Macapagal-Arroyo and,
     64–65
   growth of, 65, 79
   "holiday economics," 64–65
   independence and, 56
   logging industry, 33
   Makati region, *12*
   Manila and, 77
   manufacturing, 82–83
   mining, 33, 82
   service industry, 83
   tourism, 20, *21*, 31, 40, 41, 77,
     83, 84
   trade, 44, 79, 80, 81, 82
Edades, Victorio C., 104
education, 47, 48, 51, 89–91, *90*, 92,
   92
employment, 79, 83, 90, 117
endangered species, 38
English language, 74, 91, 92, *92*, 93
Episcopal Church, 98
Estrada, Joseph, 64, *64*
ethnic groups, 11, 87–88, 89
European colonization, 31, 46, 47, 48,
   49, 67, 68, 92, 103, 105, 122

European exploration, 16, 31, 45–46,
   45, *47*
Evangelicals, 95
executive branch of government. *See
   also* government.
   Benigno S. Aquino III, 27, 65, *65*,
     68, *68*
   cabinet of, 69, 71
   Corazon Aquino, 61–62, *61*, 63, 68
   corruption in, 58, 59–60, *60*, 62,
     63, 64
   elections, 52, 58, 60, 61–62, *61*,
     63, 65, 67–68, 69, 75
   Emilio Aguinaldo, 49, *50*, 133
   Ferdinand Marcos, 58, 59–60, *59*,
     61, 62, 63, 111, 133
   Fidel V. Ramos, 63–64
   Jejomar Binay, 69
   José Laurel, 54
   Manuel L. Quezon, 31, 52, *52*, 80
   Manuel Roxas, 55, 57
   offices of, 68, *68*, 77
   Ramon Magsaysay, 57–58, *57*
   role of, 67–68
   term limits, 59, 63, 68
   veto power, 72
   vice presidents, 69, *69*, 71

F
families, 65, 79, 89, 96, *116*, 117, *120*,
   122, 126, *126*, 127
Felipe, Julian, 74
"Filipinas" (José Palma), 74
Filipino language, 91, 92, 93
film industry, 113, *113*
fishing industry, 81, *81*
folk dance, 106, *106*, 107
foods, 35, 37, 40, 79, 81, 96, 101,
   119–120, *119*, *120*, 125
Fort Santiago, 49, *49*
Fuentes, Jovita, 110
funerals, 123, 124–125, *124*

G

Garcia, Carlos, 58
geckos, 39
geography
    caves, 23, 43, 84
    coastline, 8, 9, 16, *16*, 17, *17*, 19,
        21, *21*, 84, 84
    earthquakes, 26, *27*, 29, 30, 63
    elevation, 17, 19
    lakes, 15, 17, 22
    land area, 16, 17, 18
    landslides, 28, *28*
    mountains, 9, 15, 17, *18*, 19–20, 31
    rivers, 17, 22, 23
    volcanoes, 22, *22*, 28, 29–30, *29*,
        30, 63, 78
    waterfalls, 23, *23*, 32
giant golden-crowned flying foxes, 37
Glee television show, *109*
government. *See also* executive branch
    of government.
    agriculture and, 58, 69
    climate and, 35
    Congress of the Philippines, 58, 70
    conservation and, 72
    constitutions, 59–60, 63, 67
    Court of Appeals, 73
    elections, 66, 70–71, 72, 73, 75,
        117
    English language and, 92
    House of Representatives, 31, 70,
        71–72, 77, 114
    independence, 11, 31, 49, 50, *50*,
        53, 55, 56, 57, 67, 76, 107, 111,
        112
    Islamic religion and, *100*
    Japan and, 53–54, *53*, 67
    Judicial and Bar Council, 72
    judicial branch, 71, 72–73, 77
    laws, 72
    legislative branch, 31, 58, 63,
        70–72, 114

    local government, 69, 73
    mangrove forests and, 35
    martial law, 59, 60
    military, 59, 60, 67
    People Power Revolution, 62, 72,
        111
    political parties, 68, 75, *75*
    religion and, *100*
    Senate, 31, 70–72, 77
    Spain and, 11, 47, 48, 49, 50, 67
    Supreme Court, 72
    tsunamis and, 27
    United States and, 11, 50–53, 56,
        59, 60, 62–63, 67, 74
Guinsaugon, 28, *28*

H

halo-halo (dessert), 120
health care, 47, 69
Hinduism, 101
historical maps. *See also* maps.
    Spanish Exploration and
        Colonization, *47*
    World War II in the Philippines,
        54
holidays
    national, 107, 124, *124*, 125
    religious, 95–97, *96*, 98, 101, *101*
Homma, Masaharu, 55
House of Representatives, 31, 70,
    71–72, 77, 114
housing, *18*, *25*, 26, *26*, 30, 76, 86, 87,
    117, 118
Hukbalahap Rebellion, 56, *56*, 57
Hundred Islands National Park, 23

I

'Id al-Fitr holiday, 101
Ifugao region, 44, 86
Iglesia ni Cristo (Church of Christ),
    98–99
Iloilo City, 85

Iloilo Island, 88
imams (Muslim religious leaders), 123
independence, 11, 31, 49, 50, *50*, 53,
    55, 56, 57, 67, 76, 107, 111, 112
indigenous groups, 70
Islamic religion, 44, 47, 59, 64, 73, 88,
    95, 100–101, *100*, 105, 123

J

jai alai (sport), 115
Japan, 53–54, *53*, *54*, 55, 67
jeepneys, 85, *85*
Joaquin, Nick, 112
Judicial and Bar Council, 72
judicial branch of government, 71,
    72–73, 77

K

Katipunan group, 49
king cobras, 38
Kirov Ballet (Russia), 108
kulintang (musical instrument), *110*,
    111

L

Laguna de Bay, 17, 22, *81*
Laguna province, 88
Lake Lanao, 22
Lanao region, 88
languages, 74, 91–93, *91*, *92*, 127
La Revolucion Filipina (ballet), 107
Latin alphabet, 92, 93
Laurel, José, 54
Legarda, Loren, 72, *72*
Legazpi City, 47
Legazpi, Miguel López de, 46, 49, 76
legislative branch of government, 31,
    58, 63, 70–72, 114
Lelis, Janela Arcos, 13, *13*
Leyte Island
    Douglas MacArthur on, 54
    Guinsaugon, 28, *28*

location of, 18
Ormoc City, 26, *26*
Super Typhoon Haiyan, 28
Tropical Storm Thelma, 28
Visayan people on, 88
Leyte province, 24
Liberal Party, 68, 75
literacy rate, 48
literature, 111–112, 133
livestock, 37, *37*, 80, 118
local government, 73
Locsin, Agnes, 107
logging industry, 33
López de Villalobos, Ruy, 16
Luna, Juan, 103–104, 133
"Lupang Hinirang" (national
    anthem), 74
Lurzano, Frank, 13
Luzon group, 18, 70
Luzon Island
    Aeta people, *42*, 43
    agriculture on, 20, 44
    Bataan Peninsula, 54
    Cagayan River, 22
    Callao Cave, 43
    Caraballo Mountains, *18*, 19
    Cordillera Central mountain
        chain, 19
    housing on, *18*, 86
    Hukbalahap Rebellion, 56, *56*
    Ifugao region, 44, 86
    Laguna de Bay, 17, 22, *81*
    land area, 17
    location of, 18
    Main Crater Lake, 22, *22*
    Mayon Volcano, 28, *78*
    mining on, 82
    Pampanga River, 22
    Philippine crocodiles on, 38
    Quezon City, 31, 70, 77, 87, 98
    Taal Lake, 22, *22*
    Taal Volcano, 22, *22*, 28

Typhoon Juaning, 13
Vulcan Point Island, 22, *22*
Zambales Mountains, 19
Luzon Strait, 15

M

Macapagal-Arroyo, Gloria, 64
Macapagal, Diosdado, 58
MacArthur, Douglas, 54
Mactan-Cebu International Airport,
    85
Mactan Island, 45
Macuja-Elizalde, Lisa, *107*, 108, 133
Magellan, Ferdinand, 31, 45, *45*, 46
Magellan's Cross, 31, *31*
Magsaysay, Ramon, 57–58, *57*
Maguindanao people, 88
Main Crater Lake, 22, *22*
Malacañang Palace, 68, *68*, 77
Malay people, 11, 87
Malinao, 13
Manalo, Eduardo, 98
Manalo, Felix, 98
mangrove trees, 34–35
Manila. *See also* cities.
    Binondo neighborhood, 77
    Caloocan and, 31, 87
    children in, *127*
    Chinatown, 77
    churches in, *122*
    Clark International Airport, 85
    climate of, 17, 23
    economy and, 77
    establishment of, 46, 55
    executive branch in, 68, *68*, 77
    housing in, 76
    independence and, 76
    jeepneys in, 85, *85*
    Joseph Estrada and, 64, *64*
    judicial branch in, 72, 77
    legislative branch in, 31, 77
    Makati region, *12*

Malacañang Palace, 68, *68*, 77
Manila Metropolitan Theater, 110
Manuel L. Quezon and, 31
manufacturing in, 82–83
map of, *77*
Marikina Shoe Museum, 60, 63
marketplace in, 76
mayor of, 64, *64*
Metropolitan Manila, 76, 77,
    82–83, *84*, 85, 87, 88, *91*
Metropolitan Museum of Manila,
    104
Ninoy Aquino International
    Airport, 85
Pasay, 70
Pasig River, 76
Philippine Revolution in, 49
population of, 31, 58, 76, 87
port of, 85
Quezon City, 70, 76, 77, 87, 98
Ramadan in, *101*
Rizal Park, 90, *105*
roadways in, 85
Spanish colonization and, 76
tourism in, 77, 83
transportation in, 9, 85, *85*
Manila Bay, 22
Manila Metropolitan Theater, 110
manufacturing, 82–83
maps. *See also* historical maps.
    ethnic groups, 89
    geopolitical, *10*
    Manila, *77*
    population density, 88
    regions, *73*
    resources, 83
    Ring of Fire, *30*
    topographical, *17*
Maranao people, 88
Marcos, Ferdinand, 58, 59–60, *59*, 61,
    62, 63, 111, 133
Marcos, Imelda, 60, *60*, 63, *63*

Marikina Shoe Museum, *60, 63*
Marinduque Island, *118*
marine life, 40–41, *40, 41*, 120
marriages, 122–123, *122*
martial law, 59
Masbate Island, 18
Mayon Volcano, 28, 78
merienda (snack), 120
metric system, 80
Metropolitan Manila, 76, 77, 82–83, *84, 85, 87, 88, 91*
Metropolitan Museum of Manila, 104
military, 59, 60, 67
Mindanao Island
    Agusan River, 22
    Butig Mountains, 19
    Davao City, 31, 85, 87
    Diwata Mountains, 19
    Islamic religion on, 47
    Lake Lanao, 22
    mining on, 82
    Moro people on, 88
    Mount Apo, 17, 19, *19*, 31
    Mount Dulang-dulang, 19
    size of, 18
    T'boli people, *11*
    Tropical Storm Washi, 28
    tsunamis in, 27, 28
    Typhoon Bopha, 28
Mindanao group, 70
Mindoro Island, 18, 36
mining, 33, 82
monsoons, 23
Moro people, 59, 63, 64, 65, 88, 101, 105
Mount Apo, 17, 19, *19*, 31
Mount Dulang-dulang, 19
Mount Pinatubo volcano, 29–30, *29, 30, 63*
Mount Pulag, 19
movies, 113, *113*
music, 108–111, *108, 109, 110*, 133, *133*
Muslims. *See* Islamic religion.

N
narra trees, 33
national anthem, 74
national bird, 39, *39*
national dish, 119, 121, *121*
national flag, 13, *13*, 70, *70*
national folk dance, *106*
national holidays, 107, 124, *124*, 125
Nationalist Party, 75
Nationalist People's Coalition, 75
National Museum of the Philippines, 77, *77*
national name, 16
national parks, 23, *23*
Negros Island, 18, *32*
newspapers, 13, 93
New Year's holidays, 124, *124*
Ninoy Aquino International Airport, 85
Nixon, Richard, 59

O
opera, 110
orchids, 34
Ormoc City, 26, *26*

P
Pacific Ocean, 15, 29
Pacquiao, Emmanuel "Manny," 114, *114*, 133
Pagsanjan Gorge National Park, 23, *23*
Palawan Island, 8, *14*, 18, 23, *104*
Palma, José, 74
pamanhikan (marriage proposal), 123
Pampanga River, 22
Panay Island, 18
Pasay, 70
Pasig River, 76
Passion of Christ, 97
Passion Play, 97, *97*
Pempengco, Charice, *109*

people
    Aeta people, *42, 43*
    births, 123, *123*
    Callao Man, *42, 43*
    Cebuano Visayan people, 87
    children, 89–90, *89, 90*, 92, *92*, 96, 105–106, 115, *115, 116*, 118, *118*, 123, *123*, 126, *127*
    Chinese, 44
    clothing, 101, 123, 126, *126*
    early settlers, 43–44
    education, 47, 48, 51, 89–91, *90*, 92, *92*
    emigration, 88–89, *89*
    ethnic groups, 11, 87–88, 89
    families, 65, 79, 89, 96, 116, 117, *120*, 122, 126, *126*, 127
    foods, 35, 37, 40, 79, 81, 96, 101, 119–120, *119, 120*, 125
    friendliness of, 127, *127*
    funerals, 123, 124–125, *124*
    godfathers, 117
    godmothers, 117
    gratitude of, 117
    health care, 47, 69
    hospitality of, 127
    housing, 18, 25, 26, *26*, 30, 76, 86, 87, 117, 118
    immigration, 31
    indigenous groups, 70
    jobs, 79, 83, 90, 117
    languages, 74, 91–93, *91, 92*, 127
    literacy rate, 48, 51
    Maguindanaos, 88
    Malays, 11, 87
    Maranaos, 88
    marriages, 122–123, *122*
    Moros, 59, 63, 64, 65, 88, 101, 105
    patriotism of, 13
    population, 9, 31, 76, 87, 88
    rural areas, 118
    Samals, 88

Tagalogs, 87–88
Tausugs, 88
T'bolis, *11*
urban areas, 118
Visayans, 88
voting rights, 52, 75, 117
women, 52, 126
Yakans, 88
People Power Revolution, 62, 72, 111
pesos (currency), 41
Philip II, king of Spain, 16, *16*
Philippine-American War, *51*
Philippine Basketball Association
    (PBA), 114
Philippine crocodiles, 38, *38*
Philippine eagles, 39, *39*
Philippine falconets, 39
Philippine Idol television show, 109
Philippine Independent Church, 95,
    98
Philippine Institute of Volcanology
    and Seismology, *27*
Philippine National Games, 115
Philippine New Year, 124
Philippine peso (currency), 41, 80, *80*
Philippine Philharmonic Orchestra, 110
Philippine Revolution, 49, 98
Philippine Sea, 15
plant life
    animism, 100
    climate and, 33
    coconut palm trees, 35, *35*
    forests, 33, 34–35
    logging industry and, 33
    mangrove trees, 34–35
    mountains, 33
    narra trees, 33
    orchids, 34
    rain forests, 33
    rattan, 33
    volcanic activity and, 33
political parties, 68, 75, *75*

pollution, 87
polo, 115
population, 9, 31, 76, 87, 88
port cities, 85
Portuguese exploration, 46
pottery making, 103
Protestantism, 99
Puerto Princesa Subterranean River
    National Park, 23
pygmy falcons. *See* Philippine
    falconets.
pythons, 38

Q
Quezon City. *See also* cities.
    Ateneo de Manila University, 31
    as capital city, 31, 77
    Central Temple, 98
    founding of, 31
    legislative branch in, 31, 70
    location of, 31, 76
    name of, 31
    population of, 31, 87
    University of the Philippines
        Diliman, 31
Quezon, Manuel L., 31, 52, *52*, 80
Quirino, Elpidio, 57

R
railways, 84, 85
rainfall, 23, 24, *24*
Ramadan, 101, *101*
Ramos, Fidel V., 63–64
rattan, 33
recipe, 121, *121*
religion
    All Saints' Day, 97, *97*
    animism, 100
    Baha'i, 101
    Bathala (god), 100
    Buddhism, 101
    Central Temple, 98

Christmas holiday, 95–96, *96*
church attendance, 95
Church of England, 98
Church of the Holy Child, 31
early settlers, 44
Easter holiday, 96–97
education and, 90–91
Episcopal Church, 98
Evangelical Christians, 95
funerals and, 125
government and, *100*
Hinduism, 101
holidays, 95–97, *96*, 98, 101, *101*
Iglesia ni Cristo (Church of
    Christ), 98–99
imams (Muslim religious leaders),
    123
Islam, 44, 47, 59, 64, 73, 88, 95,
    100–101, *100*, 105, 123
Magellan's Cross, 31, *31*
marriage and, 122, *122*, 123
Mass, 95, 96, 125
Passion of Christ, 97
Passion Play, 97, *97*
People Power Revolution and, 62
Philippine Independent Church,
    95, 98
Protestantism, 99
Ramadan, 101, *101*
Roman Catholicism, 46, 47, 90–91,
    94 , 95–97, 98, 100–101, 122,
    125
Spanish colonization and, 47
Spanish exploration and, 45
split-Christianity, 100
United States and, 99
Repertory Philippines Children's
    Theatre, 105–106
reptilian life, 37–39, *38*, *40*
resorts, 21, *21*, 84
rice, 44, 78, 119
Ring of Fire, 29, *30*

Rizal, José, 48, *48*, 49, *105*, 111, 133
Rizal Park, 90, *105*
Rizal Shrine, 49
roadways, 84–85, *118*
Roman Catholicism, 46, 47, 90–91, 94, 95–97, 98, 100–101, 122, 125
Roxas, Manuel, 55, 57

S

Salonga, Lea, 108, *108*, 133, *133*
Samal people, 88
Samar Island, 18, 88
sampaguita (national flower), 34, *34*
San Fernando, 55
sarus cranes, 39, *39*
scuba diving, 41
sea turtles, *40*, 41
Senate, 31, 70–72, 77
service industry, 83
Service (movie), 113
shells, 41, *41*
sipa (sport), 115
South China Sea, 15
Spanish-American War, 49–50
Spanish colonization, 11, 31, 46, *47*, 48, 49, *49*, 67, 68, 76, 92, 103, 105, 122
Spanish exploration, 16, 31, 45–46, *45*, *47*
split-Christianity, 100
sports, 41, 114–115, *114*, 133
Sulu Island, 47, 88
Sulu Sea, 15, 41
Super Typhoon Haiyan, 24–25, *25*, 28, 35, 65
Supreme Court, 72

T

Taal Lake, 22, *22*
Taal Volcano, 22, *22*, 28
Tacloban, 24
Tagalog language, 74, 91–92, *91*, 92–93, 127

Tagalog people, 87–88
tamaraws, 36
tarsiers, 36, *36*
Tausug people, 88
T'boli people, *11*
Team PNoy coalition, *75*
television, 72, 109, 118
tenant farmers, 56
terrace farming, 20, *20*, 44, *44*, 79, 80
theater, 105–106, *105*, 108
Tojo, Hideki, 53
tourism, 20, *21*, 31, 40, 41, 77, 83, 84
towns. *See also* cities; villages.
    Capas, 55
    governments in, 73
    Malinao, 13
    music in, 108
    population of, 87
    sports in, 114, 115
    typhoons, 24
trade, 44, 79, 80, 81, 82
transportation, 9, 84–85, *84*, *85*, *116*, 118
Treaty of Paris, 50
tropical cyclones. *See* typhoons.
tropical storms, 25–26, 28
tsunamis, 26–27, 28
Tubbataha Reef National Marine Park, 41
typhoons, 13, *13*, 24–26, *24*, *25*, 28, 35, 65, *65*

U

United Nationalist Alliance, 75
United States
    Benigno S. Aquino Jr. and, 61
    education and, 51
    Ferdinand Marcos and, *59*, 62–63
    Filipino immigrants in, 88
    government and, 11, 50–53, 56, *59*, 60, 62–63, 67, 74
    Hukbalahap Rebellion and, 56
    independence and, 50, 52–53

    jeepneys and, 85
    literature and, 111
    national anthem and, 74
    Philippine-American War, *51*
    Protestantism and, 99
    Spanish-American War, 49
    tourism and, 83
    Treaty of Paris, 49–50
University of the Philippines Diliman, 31

V

villages. *See also* cities; towns.
    barangays (village committees), 73
    Guinsaugon, 28, *28*
    life in, 118
Visayan people, 88
Visayas group, 18, 20, *32*, 31, 54, 70, 84, 85
Voice of the Philippines television show, 109
Vulcan Point Island, 22, *22*

W

water buffalo, 37, *37*
waterfalls, 23, *23*, 32
weaving, *102*, 103
weights and measures, 80
wildlife. *See* animal life; marine life; plant life; reptilian life.
women, 52, 126
World War II, 49, 53–54, *53*, *54*, 55, 67

Y

Yakan people, 88

Z

Zambales Mountains, 19

Meet the Author

WALTER OLEKSY HAS BEEN A writer his entire life, from the time he was writing for the school newspaper in elementary school. He worked at the paper at Michigan State University and then became the editor of a U.S. Army paper during a stint in the military. After leaving the army, he became a newspaper reporter, eventually landing at the Chicago Tribune. He has also been a magazine writer and editor. Oleksy has written dozens of books, including books about robots and computers and biographies of Charlie Chaplin, James Dean, and Princess Diana. He has also written novels for children, including *If I'm Lost, How Come I Found You?*, which was made into a TV movie. Oleksy lives near Chicago, Illinois, with his dog, Annie.

Photo Credits

Photographs ©:

cover: Peter Adams/Jon Arnold Images/Superstock, Inc.; back cover: Dudarev Mikhail/Shutterstock, Inc.; 2: Per-Andre Hoffmann/Getty Images; 5: Tom Cockrem/Getty Images; 6 left: age fotostock/Superstock, Inc.; 6 right: Bjarki Reyr/Superstock, Inc.; 6 center: David Noton Photography/Alamy Images; 7 right: Per-Andre Hoffmann/age fotostock; 7 left: Ted Aljibe/Getty Images; 8: Travel Pix Collection/Superstock, Inc.; 11: Robert Harding Picture Library Ltd/Alamy Images; 12: Timothy Piya Trepetch/Alamy Images; 13: DanielBendjy/iStockphoto; 14: Per-Andre Hoffmann/Getty Images; 16 top: Peter Horree/Alamy Images; 16 bottom: Design Pics Inc./Alamy Images; 17: Bong Manayon/Getty Images; 18: Danita Delimont/Getty Images; 19: Hemis.fr/Superstock, Inc.; 20 top: LOOK-foto/Superstock, Inc.; 20 bottom, 21: age fotostock/Superstock, Inc.; 22: Guido Alberto Rossi/age fotostock; 23: LOOK Die Bildagentur der Fotografen GmbH/Alamy Images; 24: Sherbien Dacalanio/Alamy Images; 25: Ted Aljibe/Getty Images; 26: Ernie Sarmiento/AP Images; 27: epa european pressphoto agency b.v./Alamy Images; 28 left: Alberto Marquez/AP Images; 28 right: Lucy Pemoni/AP Images; 29: Hoa-Qui/Science Source; 30: Bruce Gordon/Getty Images; 31: LatitudeStock/Superstock, Inc.; 32: David Noton Photography/Alamy Images; 34: ntdanai/Shutterstock, Inc.; 35: Tim Graham/Alamy Images; 36: Edwin Verin/Shutterstock, Inc.; 37: Bluegreen Pictures/Alamy Images; 38: WILDLIFE GmbH/Alamy Images; 39 top: Jim Tuten/age fotostock; 39 bottom: Edwin Verin/Shutterstock, Inc.; 40: Minden Pictures/Superstock, Inc.; 41 bottom: WaterFrame/Alamy Images; 41 top: LOOK Die Bildagentur der Fotografen GmbH/Alamy Images; 42: Time & Life Pictures/Getty Images; 44: Jon Arnold Images Ltd/Alamy Images; 45: John Borthwick/Getty Images; 46: DeAgostini/Superstock, Inc.; 48: Getty Images; 49: Steve Vidler/Alamy Images; 50: Getty Images; 51: Hulton Archive/Getty Images; 52: Library of Congress; 53: AP Images; 55: Everett Collection/Superstock, Inc.; 56, 57: Time & Life Pictures/Getty Images; 58: The Granger Collection; 59: Gamma-Keystone/Getty Images; 60: epa european pressphoto agency b.v./Alamy Images; 61: Gamma-Rapho/Getty Images; 62: Sadayuki Mikami/AP Images; 63: Kyodo/AP Images; 64: AFP/Getty Images; 65: epa european pressphoto agency b.v./Alamy Images; 66: Getty Images; 68 top: Henry Westheim Photography/Alamy Images; 68 bottom: Bloomberg/Getty Images; 69: AFP/Getty Images; 70: Kheng Guan Toh/Dreamstime; 72: FRANCIS R. MALASIG/EPA/Newscom; 75: epa european pressphoto agency b.v./Alamy Images; 76 left: donsimon/Shutterstock, Inc.; 76 right: Tips Images/Tips Italia Srl a socio unico/Alamy Images; 77: Stefano Paterna/Alamy Images; 78: Per-Andre Hoffmann/age fotostock; 80: qvist/Shutterstock, Inc.; 81: Asia Images/Superstock, Inc.; 84 top: V H/age fotostock; 84 bottom, 85: Robert Harding Picture Library/Superstock, Inc.; 86: NORMA JOSEPH/Alamy Images; 89: David Grossman/Alamy Images; 90: Christian Klein/Alamy Images; 91: Mario Babiera/Alamy Images; 92: Marc F. Henning/Alamy Images; 93: Environmental Images/age fotostock; 94: Bjarki Reyr/Superstock, Inc.; 96: AFP/Getty Images; 97 top: Aaron Favila/AP Images; 97 bottom: Marc F. Henning/Alamy Images; 99: AFP/Getty Images; 100: ZUMA Press, Inc./Alamy Images; 101: epa european pressphoto agency b.v./Alamy Images; 102: Mark Floro/age fotostock; 104: Ivoha/Alamy Images; 105: Greg Elms/Getty Images; 106 top: Cheryl Ravelo/Reuters; 106 bottom: mark downey/Alamy Images; 107: A.J. SISCO UPI Photo Service/Newscom; 108: JM11 WENN Photos/Newscom; 109: Everett Collection Inc/Alamy Images; 110: Eli Ritchie Tongo/Alamy Images; 111: AFP/Getty Images; 112: J Gerard Seguia/Demotix/Corbis Images; 113: Sky Island Films/Everett Collection; 114: Hu wencheng - Imaginechina/AP Images; 115: Marc F. Henning/Alamy Images; 116: David Noton Photography/Alamy Images; 118: Robert Harding Picture Library/Superstock, Inc.; 119: Travel Pictures/Alamy Images; 120: Noli C. Gabilo/age fotostock; 121: Frances Roberts/Alamy Images; 122: Greg Elms/Getty Images; 123: Colin Utz/Alamy Images; 124 bottom: Bullit Marquez/AP Images; 124 top: AFP/Getty Images; 126 top: Deddeda/age fotostock; 126 bottom: Marc F. Henning/Alamy Images; 127: Ted Aljibe/Getty Image.

Maps by XNR Productions, Inc.